a guide to growing
perfect perennials

a guide to growing
perfect perennials

Richard Bird

LORENZ BOOKS

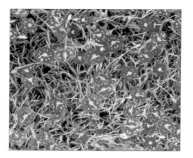

This edition published by Lorenz Books
an imprint of Anness Publishing Limited
Hermes House 88-89 Blackfriars Road
London SE1 8HA

www.lorenzbooks.com

Published in the USA by Lorenz Books
Anness Publishing Inc., 27 West 20th Street, New York, NY 10011

This edition distributed in Canada by Raincoast Books
9050 Shaughnessy Street, Vancouver, British Columbia, V6P 6E5.

A CIP catalogue record for this book is available from the British Library

Publisher: Joanna Lorenz
Senior Editor: Caroline Davison
Copy Editor: Lydia Darbyshire
Designer: Ian Sandom
Photographer: Jonathan Buckley
Production Controller: Joanna King

Jacket
Design and Art Direction: Clare Reynolds *Front cover image:* Flowers & Foliage Picture Library/Carol Sharp

© Anness Publishing Limited 1999, 2001

Previously published as *Perennials,* and as part of a larger compendium, *Annuals & Perennials*

1 3 5 7 9 10 8 6 4 2

Half title page: Black-eyed Susan (*Rudbeckia fulgida*).
Frontispiece top left: A spring border with primulas and forget-me-nots (*Myosotis*).
Frontispiece top right: A border of bright bold colours.
Frontispiece bottom left: A waterside planting, including *Rodgersia*.
Frontispiece bottom right: A late summer border, filled with perennials.
Title page: Sisyrinchiums with their striking, creamy flowers.
Above: Pinks (*Dianthus)* are ideal for a cottage garden.
Opposite: Red-hot pokers (*Kniphofia*).

CONTENTS

INTRODUCTION

If we think about the most beautiful gardens we have seen, the feature they nearly all have in common is the colours of the perennial plants. There is, of course, a structural element, provided by trees and shrubs, but it is the perennials that give these gardens their vitality and, more often than not, their originality.There are, literally, thousands of different perennial plants, offering gardeners a palette of colours, as well as a range of textures and shapes, that would make an artist envious. This choice means that gardeners can create a unique garden that reflects their own tastes. While more experienced gardeners may include the ever-increasing number of varieties now available, less experienced gardeners can still create wonderful gardens, simply by using some of the reliable plants that have stood the test of time.

The expression "perennial plants" is rather imprecise. In theory it includes all plants that do not die after they have flowered. In practice, however, trees, shrubs, rock garden plants, and tropical and tender plants are usually excluded. Instead, perennials are usually regarded as plants that die back, either completely or partially, to ground level but that reappear the following year. They are sometimes also referred to as "herbaceous plants", but this term excludes those that do not completely die back, such as pinks (*Dianthus*), some irises and red-hot pokers (*Kniphofia*). Another term that is often used is "hardy perennials", which excludes those plants such as pelargoniums that are perennials only in warmer climates and have to be treated as annuals in colder areas.

Above: *Canna leaves act as a backdrop for the climber,* Rhodochiton atrosanguineus.

Opposite: *Garden borders will reward the care and attention that you lavish on them.*

DESIGNING WITH PERENNIALS

Choosing a Scheme

One of the great advantages of using perennial plants in the garden is their versatility. The same basic selection of plants can be arranged in several ways to produce quite different results. In each situation, a plant will combine with its neighbours and take on the character of the scheme. Lady's mantle (*Alchemilla mollis*), for example, has a wonderfully old-fashioned look when combined with other such plants in a cottage garden. In a more formal arrangement, it can be used to provide an even block of yellowish-green, and, when it is grown near water, it takes on an entirely new character.

PERENNIAL USES
The versatility of perennials provides gardeners with the means to create whatever kind of garden appeals to them. Perennials can be planted in precise patterns, whereby symmetrical blocks of colour and shape are used to create a formal garden, while, at the other end of the spectrum, they can be allowed to run riot in the controlled chaos of a cottage garden. Between the two extremes is the herbaceous border, where the essential freedom of the cottage garden is married with the conscious arrangement of plants in the formal garden to create a bed that is very pleasing to the eye.

THE RIGHT PERENNIAL
Although perennial plants are versatile and, on the whole, forgiving, it is essential that when you plan your garden, whatever the proposed style, you bear in mind the origins of the plants you wish to include. Plants always grow best in conditions that are similar to their natural habitat. An extreme example is pond plants, which are unlikely to grow in dry sand. In this case, the need to match the plant's location in the garden to its natural habitat will be obvious to most gardeners. However, many gardeners fail to consider the more subtle aspects of a plant's origins. For example, plants that naturally grow in full sun rarely do well in shady conditions, and nearly all the silver-leaved plants, which love the sun, will languish and die if planted in shade.

The design of your garden must, therefore, take into consideration the type of conditions that prevail in your local area. Most of the brightly coloured flowers appear on plants that grow in direct sun, for instance, whereas woodland or shade planting relies on less colourful subjects and is more dependent on shapes, texture and the subtle colour variations of foliage.

While it is true that plants are best grown in conditions that are similar to those to which they are used in the wild, there is no reason why the conditions in your garden cannot be changed – to some extent, at least – to suit the plants you want to grow. For example, many plants like deep, rich soil, so it is hopeless trying to grow them on a light, sandy soil. However, with effort, the conditions can be altered by adding plenty of well-rotted organic material, so that these plants can be grown.

The key to using perennials is to work with, rather than against, nature, because this is much more likely to produce satisfactory results.

Above: *The fresh, bright colours of these stream-side plants make for a very attractive planting association. The jumbled colours create an informal effect.*

Above: *Contrasting flowers and foliage produce an interesting picture. Here, the foaming flowers of lady's mantle (*Alchemilla mollis*) with the green, infertile fronds and the brown, fertile fronds of the royal fern (*Osmunda regalis*) create a perfect contrast, which is ideal for a formal or informal setting.*

Above right: *Try to blend the colours of foliage and flowers. Here, the silky, silver leaves of* Stachys byzantina *and the soft, bluish-purple flowers of* Nepeta × faassenii *combine to create a soft romantic image.*

Right: *This is a perfect example of the jumble of shapes, sizes and colours that produces the informality of the cottage garden.*

Cottage Gardens

Many people regard the traditional cottage garden as the epitome of beauty, a wonderful mixture of plants that seems to spill out in all directions. Indeed, such gardens often look as if the planting is out of control and the plants have been dotted here and there, seemingly at random. Cottage gardens may have looked like this a century ago, but today many gardeners are much more design-conscious in their approach and prefer to impose some form of discipline.

COTTAGE GARDEN STYLE

In the true cottage garden, plants were positioned where there was room, and there seemed to be no organization or overall design, with the resulting effect being a riot of plants and colour. The plants were situated close together, and any gaps were soon filled by self-seeded plants, again appearing at random. The tightness of the planting had the advantage of preventing weeds from surviving or even germinating, thus reducing the amount of work involved.

Modern cottage gardens, however, are rather more organized than the traditional ones. For example, species and varieties are kept together in clumps, rather than dotted about in a haphazard way. There is a tendency to ensure that the adjacent colours of the perennials blend with each other, rather than clash – we seem to be much more colour-conscious than our ancestors used to be. There is also more control in terms of the positioning of the plants, so that the smaller ones are at the front of the border and the taller ones are at the back.

That said, however, there is no reason why you should not let things run riot, if you so wish, and create a truly old-fashioned cottage garden.

OLD-FASHIONED PERENNIALS

One of the elements that gives the cottage garden its particular atmosphere is the use of "old-fashioned" plants, which may be described as plants that were grown by our ancestors and that are still grown today, largely unchanged. Apart from aesthetic reasons, there are other grounds for growing old-fashioned plants. The most important is that these plants have survived because they are tough. They are sufficiently resistant to the weather, pests and diseases to have lasted for several centuries. This means that many of them are relatively free of problems, making gardeners' lives easier.

Another reason for the enduring popularity of old-fashioned perennials is their appearance: they are, quite simply, attractive. They may not have the big, blowsy flowers in bold, bright colours that many modern plant breeders would have us like, but they are, nonetheless, usually covered in glorious flowers, often in subtle pastel shades, with occasional splashes of bright colour to liven up the border.

Modern plant breeding has concentrated so much on size and colour that scent has almost been bred out of many flowers. One advantage of the species and old varieties found in traditional cottage gardens is that they are often highly perfumed, an important quality in the make-up of a romantic cottage garden.

Left: *Spring in the cottage garden heralds the appearance of primulas, forget-me-nots, columbines and bluebells; all of these perennials are firm favourites with those who adopt this ever-popular style of gardening.*

Above: *A typical cottage garden path with plants spilling over it. The plants, such as the foxgloves (*Digitalis purpurea*) shown here, are allowed to self-seed where they like.*

Above: *The tight planting of a cottage garden allows little room for weeds to grow. Here, a mixture of self-sown annuals and planted perennials creates a wonderfully relaxed picture.*

Above: *Columbines (*Aquilegia*) contrast with the filmy foliage of fennel (*Foeniculum vulgare*).*

Above: *Greater masterwort (*Astrantia major*) has a lovely, old-fashioned quality that makes it a perfect subject for including in a cottage garden.*

COTTAGE GARDEN PERENNIALS

Alcea rosea (hollyhock)
Anemone × hybrida (Japanese anemone)
Aquilegia vulgaris (granny's bonnet)
Aster novae-angliae; *A. novi-belgii*
Astrantia major (masterwort)
Bellis perennis (double daisy)
Campanula persicifolia; *C. portenschlagiana;* *C. poscharskyana*
Centaurea cyanus (cornflower); *C. montana* (perennial cornflower)
Chrysanthemum
Delphinium
Dianthus (carnations, pinks)
Dicentra spectabilis (bleeding heart, Dutchman's trousers)
Doronicum (leopard's bane)
Galium odoratum, syn. *Asperula odorata* (woodruff)
Geranium ibericum
Geum rivale (water avens)
Lathyrus (vetchling)
Lupinus (lupin)
Lychnis chalcedonica (Jerusalem cross, Maltese cross)
Lysimachia nummularia (creeping Jenny)
Meconopsis cambrica (Welsh poppy)
Monarda didyma (bee balm, bergamot)
Myrrhis odorata (sweet cicely)
Paeonia officinalis (peony)
Polemonium caeruleum
Primula
Pulmonaria (lungwort)
Ranunculus aconitifolius (bachelor's buttons)
Saponaria officinalis (bouncing Bet)
Sedum spectabile (ice-plant)

Formal Gardens

As the name implies, formal gardens tend to be highly organized, with each plant in its place and no chance of self-sown seedlings appearing to disrupt the design. The overall plan is based on the use of symmetry, straight lines and smooth curves. It is this combination of regular lines and carefully positioned plants that makes the formal garden so different to the cottage garden, in which it can be said that anything goes.

FORMAL EFFECTS

A strictly formal garden is designed with precise regularity. The garden itself may be square or rectangular, but there should be a set piece in the centre, as well as borders around the edges. The planting on each side of the square or rectangular garden should be mirrored on the opposite side. Certain plants may also be repeated at intervals along the borders to create a sense of rhythm.

A formal garden may take the form of a parterre, in which the borders are contained by low hedging. This may be provided by a shrubby plant, such as box (*Buxus*), or by plants like santolina or germander (*Teucrium*), which are technically shrubs or sub-shrubs, but usually regarded as perennials in the garden. Within the hedges, perennials of a uniform colour and size are set out in blocks, or a variety of plants are laid out in a pattern that is then echoed elsewhere in the design.

Not all formal gardens are symmetrical. Some schemes that may be considered formal have no real formality at all, depending more on simplicity for the effect they produce. In this type of garden the number of plants is severely restricted. There might be, for example, one or two well-chosen plants, sited in telling positions. Alternatively, there may be a formal pond, with plants in one corner – a tall reed, perhaps, or three plants, a taller one with two others in front, forming a close triangle. Other arrangements might include a single clump of tall grass or bamboo in a gravelled area.

Plants in a formal garden often play a lesser role than features such as hedges, paths, statuary, large ponds and fountains. When plants are introduced, they are often selected for their architectural qualities – a single clump of flax lily (*Phormium*), for example. A cabbage tree (*Cordyline*), with its even spread of pointed leaves, is another perfect plant for such a garden, whether planted directly in the ground or grown in a container.

Stark formality is not really the business of this book. We are more concerned with the use of perennials, and formal gardens, attractive though they often are, do not use as many different perennials as most gardeners would like. However, if you feel that a formal garden is the right choice for you, remember that there are many occasions when perennials can be organized in a formal way, while many of the plants that are suggested for less formal gardens can also be used to create an eye-catching, symmetrical scheme.

Above: *Grasses have simple, elegant shapes that rarely look fussy. This makes them suitable for formal settings, either used as single specimens or planted in groups, as is the case here.*

Above: *Foliage is often more important than flowers in a formal setting, as is demonstrated by this group that is dominated by* Euphorbia mellifera. *The coolness of the greens looks very striking in combination with the white stone planter.*

Above right: *Rhythm and repetition in a garden create a feeling of formality, as does the use of straight lines and simple shapes. The clipped box balls in this formal garden contribute to the overall effect by creating a satisfying rhythm down the length of the garden.*

Right: *This large sunken garden shows how a formal layout can be softened with well-placed plants such as lady's mantle (*Alchemilla mollis*), whose foaming, lime-green flowers are spilling out over the edges of the paths.*

Herbaceous Borders

A herbaceous border is simply a border devoted to herbaceous plants. At the end of the year all the plants die back, but then sprout anew the following spring. A large herbaceous border in full flower is a wonderful sight and more than compensates for the empty winter months when there are fewer perennials to see.

THE SIZE OF THE BORDER

In the past, herbaceous borders tended to be extensive and required the attention of a large number of gardeners. However, a successful herbaceous border need be neither large nor labour-intensive. It is perfectly true that a huge herbaceous border several hundred metres (yards) long is an incredible sight, but then so is one that extends for only about ten metres or less. Unlike the Victorians, we do not necessarily believe that the size of a border is a measure of its effectiveness. We are probably more concerned with the plants that are growing there.

When it comes to the amount of labour needed to maintain herbaceous borders, it is a mistake to think that you need a staff of full-time gardeners to ensure that they look their best. You will definitely need help if your borders are several hundred metres long, but the borders that can be accommodated in most of today's private gardens can be looked after by the owner. As long as the ground is well prepared in the first place and work is carried out early in the year, before the weeds can get a hold, herbaceous borders are easy and, in fact, pleasurable to maintain.

SEASONAL CHANGES

The winter months can be a problem for those who feel that the garden must offer something all year round. In the old days herbaceous borders were often part of a larger garden, in which there were plenty of other areas to see during the winter months, including, in the very largest gardens, tropical glasshouses!

Today, however, many gardeners are as interested in the dried remains of the perennials as they are in their appearance when in full growth. Many plants die very gracefully, and their bare, dead stems can be unexpectedly attractive. Grasses, in particular, are useful in this respect, but there are many other plants, either in clumps or as individual stems, that are eye-catching in dull, winter light. These remains also, of course, provide invaluable food and shelter for birds and insects.

CHOOSING THE COLOURS

The design of a herbaceous border is a matter of personal preference, and individual tastes can all be accommodated using the incredible range of plants now available. The perennials are usually grouped so that the colours blend harmoniously. They are often arranged so that the hotter colours are in the centre and the cooler tones at the ends of the border. It is also possible to create borders that are restricted to only one colour or to a group of colours – pastel shades or hot colours, for example. Some gardeners prefer a white border or one that is limited to plants that have yellow and blue flowers and foliage. The number of variations on these themes is almost limitless, and each offers the possibility of a border that is unique.

Below: *This is a typical layout, with twin herbaceous borders separated by a wide path. Such a planting scheme is unbeatable in midsummer.*

Above: *An informal herbaceous border that relies on both foliage and flowers for its effect, contrasting grasses and hostas with Welsh poppies* (Meconopsis cambrica) *and columbines* (Aquilegia).

Above: *A vivid contrast between the purple of this* Phlox *and the silver foliage of the* Anaphalis *brings alive this section of the border. Too much contrast, however, would create an uncomfortable effect.*

Above: *A daylily (*Hemerocallis*) peeping through the delicate, silver foliage of an* Artemisia *makes for a wonderful contrast of flower and foliage.*

Right: *Dedicated colour schemes can produce particularly striking results. Here, a gravel-edged border has been filled with perennials in a range of hot colours, creating a bright, cheerful atmosphere.*

Mixed Borders

An increase in interest in the mixed border came with the decline in popularity of the herbaceous border earlier this century. The mixed border is so-called because, of course, it contains a mixture of plants. It is not restricted solely to herbaceous plants, but can also include shrubs and even trees.

THE ADVANTAGES

Devotees prefer the mixed border to the traditional herbaceous border for several reasons. The main reason is that including trees and shrubs gives the border a clear structure and a permanent framework. Even in winter there is something to see, especially if the shrubs are evergreen. Although many herbaceous plants have a relatively long season of interest, many have only a brief one. This can be regarded as an advantage in many ways – borders that are dynamic and ever-changing make for a much more interesting garden. The sudden blooming of a clump of red flowers, for example, not only provides a point of interest, but also changes the whole appearance of the border.

The advantages of a mixed border are easier to understand if you contrast this type of border with, say, an annual bedding scheme, which remains largely the same throughout the summer and autumn.

COMBINING THE PLANTS

Some gardeners do not like too much change in the garden but prefer to have one or two anchor points that provide a permanent structure within which the perennials can be allowed to weave their constantly changing thread. In some respects, reducing the amount of change in a border emphasizes what remains.

Including trees and shrubs widens the scope of plants that can be used in a border and introduces a wider variety of shapes and textures into the overall design. In general, trees and shrubs also have a more "solid" appearance, which is important, whether they are dotted around the border, grouped together or even used as a backdrop. This structure is particularly important if there is no proper background to the border, such as a hedge or wall.

Many perennials often look their best when grown with shrubs. A clump of day lilies (*Hemerocallis*), for example, peeping out from between two shrubs, can look superb.

Another advantage of incorporating trees and shrubs into a border is that they provide shade. Although many gardeners try to avoid shade, it does provide a habitat for a wider range of perennials than could otherwise be grown in a border.

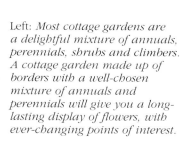

Left: *Most cottage gardens are a delightful mixture of annuals, perennials, shrubs and climbers. A cottage garden made up of borders with a well-chosen mixture of annuals and perennials will give you a long-lasting display of flowers, with ever-changing points of interest.*

Above: *Annuals, perennials and shrubs all play a part in this tightly packed planting scheme. The colours, textures and shapes of the plants are used to good effect to create an eye-catching border.*

Above: *Combining perennials with shrubs – here* Sisyrinchium striatum *is growing with* Rosa *'Félicité Perpétue' – allows for a greater variety of planting and hence a more interesting scheme than could be achieved using perennials alone.*

Right: *Some shrubs are regarded as "honorary" perennials. Herbs, such as the sage shown here, as well as lavender and rosemary, are frequently seen in association with perennials.*

Island Beds

Although they have long been a part of the bedding plant tradition, it is only relatively recently that island beds have become an acknowledged element of the perennial scene. Island beds are simply borders that you can walk around completely, and so view from all angles. They may be positioned in the centre of a lawn or within a paved area, or they can be circumnavigated by a path.

SHAPES AND SIZES

The shapes of island beds can vary enormously. In more formal gardens, the shapes should be regular, including circles, ovals and squares. However, triangles should be avoided, unless they are large, because it is difficult to plant the corners of a triangle satisfactorily, especially if they come to a sharp point.

Formal shapes do not, however, lend themselves particularly well to the informality of most perennial plants, for which larger, free-form beds are usually much more satisfactory. By this is meant a self-contained bed that has a sinuous edge. The line of the edge should not be determined at random, however, since it always looks better if it reflects the shape of a nearby border or path, or swings out around a tree or some other garden feature.

Allied to the shape is the size of the bed: a simple rule to remember is that perennial island beds should never be too small. In fact, if the shape of the bed can be taken in at a glance, the bed is probably too small. The best island beds are large enough to accommodate some tall plants, or even some trees and shrubs in the centre of the bed in order to introduce some

height. The worst beds are those in which there is not enough space for the plants to develop any height. In such beds, your eyes are likely to sweep straight across the planting to whatever lies beyond.

CHOOSING THE PERENNIALS

The idea of looking beyond the bed is an important one. When you are planning both the size and contents of the bed, always make sure that it is filled with plants of an appropriate height and density. No plant looks its best if you can see straight though it. A thin scattering of low plants usually looks unappealing and does little for the overall appearance of the garden.

One of the advantages of an island bed is that it can be sited in the open, away from the shade, with plenty of air circulating among the plants. This type of position is greatly appreciated by many sun-loving plants. In larger island beds, however, where there is a central planting of small trees and shrubs, shade will be created on one side. The shade will vary in intensity across the bed and provide an opportunity to grow a range of plants that have different growing requirements.

CREATING A CIRCULAR BED

1 Insert a post in the centre of the proposed bed. Attach one end of a piece of string to the post and the other end to a bottle filled with sand or peat.

2 Walk slowly around the post, keeping the string taut and the bottle tilted, so that the sand trickles out and marks the outline of the circle.

CREATING AN IRREGULAR BED

Use a flexible hosepipe to work out the size and shape of an irregular bed. Once you are happy with the shape of the bed, remove a line of turf around the edge of the pipe to mark it out.

CREATING AN OVAL BED

Place two posts in the ground and loosely tie a piece of string around them. Experiment with the distance between the posts and the length of the piece of string to get the size and shape of bed you require. Place a bottle filled with peat or sand inside the loop of string and walk around the posts, keeping the string taut. The sand trickles out of the bottle, creating the outline of a perfect oval.

3 Once the circle is complete, the turf can be cut from within the marked area in order to produce a perfectly circular bed.

PREPARING THE GROUND

1 With many lawn grasses, it will not be necessary to use a herbicide; simply skim off the surface grass and dig out any roots that remain.

2 Dig the soil, removing any weeds and stones. Mix in plenty of organic material as you dig to encourage the roots to grow deeply.

3 Leave the bed to weather for a few months after digging, and remove any residual weeds. Fork in well-rotted compost and rake level before planting.

Above: *This island bed is filled with an array of colourful perennials and surrounded by mown grass paths.*

Shady Plantings

Many gardeners regard areas of shade as a problem, but they can be an advantage in many ways, because they provide a greater variety of habitats, thus increasing the range of plants that can be grown. Shade is not something to worry about, as so many gardeners seem to do.

SUITABLE PERENNIALS

The golden rule when planting shady areas is to use perennials that grow naturally in the shade. If this rule is followed, you should have no difficulty in establishing a fine range of perennials. It may seem an obvious point to make, but the main reason so many gardeners dread gardening in shady areas is because they want to grow the brightly coloured plants that thrive in full sun. They plant them in shady borders, and they quickly become drawn and etiolated, as they struggle to the light; then they turn sickly because they are undernourished and short of light. This, in turn, means that they are more susceptible to disease, and, before long, the plants die. If you choose plants that like the shade, the results will be completely different.

DEGREES OF SHADE

It is important to distinguish between the different types of shade and to give your perennials the right conditions. The first kind of shade is known as light or partial shade. This includes areas that are in sun for part of the day or are lightly shaded by objects through which the sun can penetrate from time to time. The mottled light under some trees comes into this category, which also includes areas such as the north side of a building where the sun does not reach, but where there is always light from above.

Dense shade is defined as an area in which sunlight never penetrates and the low levels of light make the site gloomy. This type of shade is much more problematic. Fortunately, few gardens are entirely in dense shade, although there may be one or two small areas that are.

You can alter the level of shade in parts of the garden. If you have a large tree, for example, removing the lower branches allows more light to reach the ground beneath. The branches in the main canopy can also be thinned to create a dappled light. In a dark, north-facing area, a fence or wall opposite the site can be painted white to reflect the available light towards the shady bed.

Above: *Many hellebores, including this* Helleborus odorus, *grow well in light shade.*

Left: Geranium macrorrhizum *is one of the best perennial plants for growing in shade. Here, it is flowering well in fairly dark conditions.*

Some shade-loving perennials, such as pulmonarias and hellebores, can be planted under deciduous trees, which have lost their leaves during the perennials' main flowering season, thus providing plenty of light at the crucial time when these plants produce their flowers.

Remember, too, that the type of soil is important. Many shade-loving perennials are naturally woodland plants, and so need a woodland-like soil. This should be high in organic materials, such as leafmould, which hold plenty of moisture. Some perennials will grow in dry woodland soils – *Euphorbia amygdaloides robbiae*, for example – but for a greater range of plants it is better to modify the soil in order to create better conditions.

Above: *Both primulas and ferns relish growing in light shade. Plants always do well if given the conditions they prefer.*

Above: *Columbines are usually grown in the open border, but are frequently found in open woodland in the wild. Why not follow nature and use them in shady borders?*

SHADE-LOVING PERENNIALS

Achlys triphylla
Actaea alba (white baneberry); *A. rubra* (red baneberry)
Alchemilla mollis (lady's mantle)
Anemone nemorosa (wood anemone)
Aruncus dioicus (goat's beard)
Asarum caudatum; *A. hartwegii*
Begonia grandis evansiana (hardy begonia)
Bergenia (elephant's ears)
Brunnera macrophylla, syn. *Anchusa myosotidiflora*
Caltha palustris (kingcup, marsh marigold)
Campanula latifolia
Cardamine bulbifera; *C. enneaphyllos*; *C. kitaibelii*; *C. pentaphyllos*
Carex pendula (pendulous sedge)
Convallaria majalis (lily-of-the-valley)
Corydalis flexuosa
Dicentra
Disporum (fairy bells)
Dryopteris filix-mas (male fern)
Epimedium
Eranthis hyemalis (winter aconite)
Euphorbia amygdaloides (wood spurge); *E. amygdaloides robbiae*
Geranium (cranesbill; some)
Glaucidium palmatum
Hacquetia epipactis
Helleborus (hellebore)
Hosta
Houttuynia cordata
Iris foetidissima (stinking iris)
Jeffersonia diphylla; *J. dubia*
Kirengeshoma palmata
Lamium galeobdolon (yellow archangel)

Lathyrus vernus (spring vetchling)
Lilium martagon (Turk's cap lily)
Liriope muscari (lilyturf)
Meconopsis (blue poppy)
Milium effusum 'Aureum' (Bowles' golden grass)
Myosotis sylvatica (garden forget-me-not)
Omphalodes cappadocica; *O. verna* (blue-eyed Mary)
Oxalis acetosella (wood sorrel)
Paris (herb Paris)
Pentaglottis sempervirens
Persicaria affinis (syn. *Polygonum affine*)
Phlox divaricata (blue phlox, wild sweet William); *P. stolonifera* (creeping phlox)
Podophyllum hexandrum (syn. *P. emodi*); *P. peltatum* (May apple)
Polygonatum (Solomon's seal)
Polystichum setiferum (soft shield fern)
Primula
Pulmonaria (lungwort)
Sanguinaria canadensis (bloodroot)
Smilacina racemosa (false spikenard); *S. stellata* (star flower)
Smyrnium perfoliatum
Stylophorum
Symphytum ibericum (syn. *S. grandiflorum*)
Tellima grandiflora
Tiarella (foamflower)
Trillium (wood lily)
Uvularia (merrybells)
Vancouveria
Viola odorata (sweet violet); *V. riviniana* Purpurea Group (Labrador violet)
Waldsteinia ternata

Waterside Plantings

Water is an invaluable addition to any garden, partly because it allows a whole new range of plants and wildlife to flourish. Water in the garden also has a very soothing effect. The sound of water tinkling from a fountain or running in a stream is utterly relaxing. Watching the constantly moving reflections of sunlight, sky and the surrounding vegetation can also be wonderfully calming and almost hypnotic.

THE BENEFITS OF WATER

Water attracts wildlife, and a pond will encourage birds as well as beautiful insects, such as dragonflies and damselflies, to visit the garden. The shape of the pond is important – where a natural pond is appropriate for a wildlife garden, a pond with a rigid concrete surround is more suitable for a more formal garden.

For the gardener who is interested in perennial plants, however, the main attraction of a pond is the range of plants that it is possible to grow. A pond provides three areas for planting that are not available in a garden without water. The first area is in the water itself, which will enable you to grow a wide variety of plants such as waterlilies (*Nymphaea*). These can be planted in the mud at the bottom of a naturally occurring pond, but if your pond is lined they will have to be planted in special baskets.

The next planting is the shallow water at the edge of the pond. The plants suitable for these conditions include the beautiful *Iris laevigata* and its cultivars, which, again, can be grown in the mud or in baskets. When you are constructing a pond, it is important to create a series of tiers around the edge. This provides different planting depths, so that you can include a variety of plants, as some water plants prefer shallower conditions than others.

Finally, there are the damp margins of the pond. Many plants thrive on the shore, rather than in the water, although several of the plants that grow in shallow water will also survive in the conditions at the margins of the pond because they are used to water rising and falling in their natural habitats.

If you are building a pond with a liner, it is always a good idea to run the liner under the soil some way from the margin of the pond in order to create a damp patch. If the liner comes up to the surface right at the edge of the pond, then the soil on the bank will be too dry to grow pond plants.

Even if you do not have a pond, it is possible to create a boggy area by digging a depression, lining it with a sheet of pond liner, and filling it with a rich mixture of good soil and organic matter. Puncture a few drainage holes in the liner so that stagnant water does not accumulate. Such an area will be a lush haven of plants, even in very dry weather.

Above: *Some plants, such as these waterlilies (*Nymphaea*), will only grow in water where the leaves and flowers can float. They cannot be grown in ordinary soil or even a bog garden.*

Left: *These rodgersias are typical of many plants that like waterside conditions. They are lush, healthy, and growing well.*

WATERSIDE PERENNIALS

Aruncus (goat's beard)
Astilbe
Caltha
Cardamine (bitter cress)
Cimicifuga (bugbane)
Darmera peltata,
  syn. *Peltiphyllum peltatum*
  (umbrella plant)
Eupatorium
Filipendula
  (meadowsweet)
Gunnera
Hosta
Iris ensata, syn. *I. kaempferi*
  (Japanese water iris);
  I. sibirica
Ligularia (leopard plant)
Lobelia cardinalis
  (cardinal flower)

Lysichiton (bog arum,
  skunk cabbage)
Lysimachia (yellow loosestrife)
Lythrum (purple loosestrife)
Mimulus (monkey flower,
  musk)
Onoclea sensibilis
  (sensitive fern)
Osmunda regalis (royal fern)
Persicaria bistorta, syn.
  Polygonum bistorta
  (bistort, snakeweed)
Phragmites
Primula
Rheum (ornamental rhubarb)
Rodgersia
Trollius (globeflower)
Zantedeschia aethiopica
  (arum lily)

Above: *Waterlilies (*Nymphaea*) often form a vast raft of foliage. Like many other garden plants, there are times when they need to be kept in check.*

Above: *The arum lily,* Zantedeschia aethiopica, *is perfect for a waterside planting. It will also grow in shallow water.*

Above: *A good waterside planting in which the ebullience of the yellow mimulus contrasts well with the restrained foliage of the hosta.*

Wild Flower Plantings

In some respects all flower gardens may be described as wild flower plantings. Every plant we grow in our gardens, including the species, which are undoubtedly wild flowers, as well as the other highly bred forms that we can buy today, originated somewhere in the wild. However, the term "wild flowers" is usually taken to mean those flowers that grow wild in the local area.

WILD FLOWER HABITATS

Increasing pressure on the countryside means that the number of wild flowers is diminishing, and, unfortunately, this is a worldwide problem. One way of combating this demise is by creating wild flower habitats within our own gardens. Such areas, in turn, have the benefit of reintroducing wildlife, especially in the form of insects, such as butterflies, which thrive on the native plants, but are less happy on many of the introduced or hybridized ones that we grow in our gardens. On the whole, most wild flowers are not as attractive individually as cultivated ones, but when they are gathered together in, say, a meadow garden, their beauty becomes much more apparent.

WILD FLOWER GARDENS

One might expect growing wild plants to be fairly easy, but establishing and maintaining a wild flower garden is one of the most difficult types of gardening. There is the natural tendency, especially in cultivated ground, for the ranker weeds to take over and smother the plants you want to encourage. Success depends largely on the way you approach the task as well as on the initial preparation.

The first method is to allow wild flowers to colonize some existing grass. If this is a lawn, you should not have many problems, but if you are lucky enough to have a field, the grasses are likely to be too rank for the flowers to survive. The first task is to spend a year mowing the grass at regular intervals to keep it short. This will kill off most of the ranker grasses and leave the finer ones.

The next step, whether you have a field or a lawn, is to put in wild flower plants at random throughout the meadow. You can scatter the seed directly over the area, if you wish, but the competition is intense, and so it is better to sow the seed in trays, prick out and grow on the plants in pots first. Plant out in spring when the perennials are strong enough to compete. Once established, they will self-sow, which is always more successful than simply scattering the seed.

The second method is to clear the ground completely, removing all traces of perennial weeds. Then, sow a wild flower and grass seed mixture that has been especially formulated for your area. There are several suppliers for this type of seed. It is worth finding the right seed mixture, as it is important to use only those

perennials that already grow, or are likely to grow, in your area. These will have the best chance of surviving. For example, there is little point in trying to naturalize plants from chalk (alkaline) downland on acid heathland soil.

Once the meadow is established, it should be cut regularly, about once or twice a year, to prevent the rank weeds from taking over. The best time is usually in summer once the main flush of plants have seeded.

Above: *Here, wild flowers are growing to great effect in a herbaceous border. Evening primrose (Oenothera biennis) and feverfew (Tanacetum parthenium) make a sympathetic planting combination.*

On a much smaller scale it is also possible to create a wild flower garden simply by sowing or planting perennials along a hedgerow, which is another natural habitat in itself.

PERENNIALS FOR WILD FLOWER PLANTINGS

Achillea millefolium
(milfoil)

Ajuga reptans
(common bugle)

Asclepias tuberosa
(butterfly weed)

*Campanula
rotundifolia* (harebell)

Cardamine pratensis
(cuckoo flower,
lady's smock)

Centaurea scabiosa

Fritillaria meleagris
(snake's head fritillary;
this is a bulb)

Geranium pratense
(meadow cranesbill)

Hypericum perforatum
(St. John's wort)

Leontodon hispidus
(rough hawkbit)

Malva moschata
(musk mallow)

Monarda fistulosa
(wild bergamot)

Narcissus pseudonarcissus
(Lent Lily; this is a bulb)

Primula veris (cowslip)

Prunella vulgaris

Ranunculus acris
(meadow buttercup);
R. bulbosus (bulbous
buttercup); *R. repens*
(creeping buttercup)

Stellaria graminea
(lesser stitchwort)

Succisa pratensis
(devil's bit scabious)

Above: *A beautiful wild flower meadow edged with red valerian* (Centranthus ruber*) that is growing in an old wall.*

Above: *Many garden flowers are forms of wild flowers.* Ajuga reptans *'Catlin's Giant' is a large form of the species.*

Above: *Wild flowers can also be planted in shade.* Anemone nemorosa *and* Ranunculus auricomis *are both woodlanders.*

Container Plantings

There is a tendency to think of perennials in terms of the herbaceous border or bed, and, while it is true that they are border plants par excellence, many can also be used as container plants. As with most of the ways in which you can use perennials, the possibilities are endless, with new ideas for container plantings appearing all the time.

PERENNIALS FOR CONTAINERS

Many of the so-called "annuals" that are used in windowboxes and hanging baskets are, in fact, perennials, but most, such as pelargoniums and petunias, are tender, and are therefore treated as annuals. Others are on the borderline of hardiness and may survive mild winters, but it is the true hardy perennials that we are considering here.

On the whole, it is much more effective to plant perennials in a container as individual species or varieties, rather than using them in mixed plantings. This is partly because they look best like this, but it also has a lot to do with the size of the plants – if you have a large flax lily (*Phormium*) in a pot, there is not much room for anything else.

When plants are grown in isolation in this way, it is also much easier to appreciate them than when they are part of a busy border. For example, the fountain-like foliage of a hosta in a pot will stand out against stone or brick paving in a way that would be impossible if the same plant were surrounded by other foliage. Similarly, the spiky appearance of a cabbage tree (*Cordyline*) can also be fully appreciated in a container on a plinth, silhouetted against a plain background or the sky.

Perennials in containers can be used in a variety of ways. Placing the container in a border may seem rather odd, but this can be a good way of filling any gaps – a pot of African lilies (*Agapanthus*), for example, can be stood in the gap left when a spring-flowering plant dies back.

When they are raised on plinths, containers also work well as focal points. For example, a large container on a plinth might be placed in a border, positioned at the end of a path, or at the edge or centre of the lawn. The eye is drawn immediately to the container, and this is the perfect way to focus a visitor's attention towards – or even away from – another garden feature. Containers can also be used to great advantage in more obvious places, notably on patios, either arranged in groups or used singly to show off individual specimens.

The other great advantage of container-grown perennials is that they can be moved around to create fresh displays, and, as the flowers of one plant go over, another coming into bloom can be moved in to replace it, producing an ever-changing scene in the border.

Containers are also the ideal way of decorating or drawing attention to a flight of stairs. They can be positioned on the highest or lowest steps to guide the eye up or down. They can also be set to stand guard on each side of a doorway or arch, thus creating a well-defined entrance to the house or garden.

SUITABLE PERENNIALS FOR CONTAINERS

Acanthus (bear's breeches)
Agapanthus (African lily)
Bergenia (elephant's ears)
Cordyline (cabbage tree)
Dianthus (carnations, pinks)
Diascia
Euphorbia (spurge)
Geranium (cranesbill)
Geum
Hemerocallis (daylily)
Heuchera (coral bells)
Hosta
Iris
Nepeta
Oenothera fruticosa glauca (sundrops)
Phormium tenax (New Zealand flax)
Primula
Sedum
Stachys byzantina, syn. *S. lanata* (lamb's ears)
Verbena

Left: *The beautiful mauve flowers of* Convolvulus sabatius *complement the warm, terracotta colour of the pot. Being a slightly tender plant, the convolvulus can be moved inside in its pot for the winter.*

PLANTING A CONTAINER

1 These are the materials you will need to plant a container. They include a terracotta pot, your choice of plant (in this case, a cordyline), some stones for drainage, potting compost (soil mix), slow-release fertilizer (either loose or in pellets) and water-retaining granules.

2 Cover the bottom of the container with small stones or some pieces of tile or pottery, so that water can drain freely from the pot.

3 Partly fill the pot with a good quality potting compost. Some loose slow-release fertilizer and water-retaining granules can be mixed with the compost before filling the pot.

4 Scoop a hole in the compost and insert the plant, positioning it so that the top of the rootball will be level with the surface of the compost.

5 Place any extra plants you wish to include around the edge of the main plant. Add more compost to fill any gaps, and firm down.

6 Insert a fertilizer pellet if you have decided to use one, rather than the loose fertilizer granules. Water thoroughly.

7 The plants will soon grow away and fill out the container.

Fragrant Perennials

As you would expect from a range of plants as diverse as the perennials, there are a number that are fragrant, which adds to the enjoyment of growing them.

THE SCENTED GARDEN

It is possible to create borders especially devoted to scent, but, in many ways, it is more exciting to come across a fragrance at random. If too many fragrant plants are placed together, the various fragrances may conflict with each other, so they can be appreciated neither singly nor together. Placing scented plants judiciously around the garden, on the other hand, means that individual scents can suddenly assail you as you walk around, often before you are conscious of the plants themselves.

Although it is pleasant to come across scents as you walk along a border, it is often far more enjoyable to relax on a seat or in an arbour that has perfumed plants set near to it. This is a particularly good idea if you have a patio where you can eat on a summer's evening. Many plants are evening-scented, and sitting in the garden after a hard day's work, as the light begins to fade and the scents start to float on the warm air, is one of the most pleasant and effective ways to relax and forget the problems of the day.

A similar idea is to position scented plants near doors and windows that are likely to be open, so that the scents waft in and fill the room. Planting your favourite scented plant near to the drive so that it welcomes you as you arrive home is also a sure way to emphasize the break between work and home.

CAPTURING THE SCENT

Scent can be elusive. Sometimes it travels a long way on the air and at other times you have to place your nose in the flower before it becomes apparent. Some scents have to react with the air before they can be smelt – when you are close to the flower you cannot smell anything, but move a few feet away, and there it is.

Other scents are not given off until the plant is bruised. *Artemisia*, for example, does not smell until you gently crush its leaves. Plants of this type should be planted close to paths, so that their scent is released as you brush past them. Catmint or catnip (*Nepeta cataria*) is good for this.

You should remember that not all plants are pleasantly fragrant. Your family will not be appreciative if you plant a dragon arum (*Dracunculus vulgaris*) under a window. It is a striking plant, but put it at the bottom of the garden because it has a strong foetid smell, rather like rotten flesh, which it uses to attract flies.

Remember, too, that not everyone likes the same scents – *Phuopsis stylosa*, for example, has a foxy, rather pungent smell that some people dislike. Some scents change in character during the day – for instance, *Cestrum parqui* has a strong savoury smell during the day, but a sweet fragrance at night.

Above all, remember that while much pleasure can be obtained from scented plants, they must always be used with discretion.

Left: *Lupins have a very distinctive, peppery scent, which, like many plant perfumes, is most apparent in warm weather.*

SCENTED FLOWERS

Acorus calamus (sweet flag)
Adenophora liliifolia
Aponogeton distachyos
 (water hawthorn)
Asphodeline lutea
 (syn. *Asphodelus luteus*)
Calanthe discolor
Cestrum parqui
Chrysanthemum
Clematis heracleifolia;
 C. recta
Convallaria majalis
 (lily-of-the-valley)
Cosmos atrosanguineus
 (chocolate cosmos)
Crambe cordifolia;
 C. maritima (seakale)
Delphinium wellbyi
 (syn. *D. leroyi*)
Dianthus (carnations, pinks)
Filipendula ulmaria
Helleborus lividus
Hemerocallis citrina;
 H. dumortieri;
 H. lilioasphodelus (syn.
 H. flava); *H. middendorffii*;
 H. multiflora
Hosta 'Honeybells';
 H. plantaginea
Iris 'Florentina';
 I. germanica (common
 German flag); *I. hoogiana*;
 I. pallida dalmatica;

I. unguicularis (Algerian iris)
Lobularia maritima,
 syn. *Alyssum maritimum*
 (sweet alyssum)
Lunaria rediviva
 (perennial honesty)
Lupinus polyphyllus
Mirabilis jalapa
 (four o'clock flower)
Paeonia (peony; some)
Petasites fragrans (winter
 heliotrope); *P. japonicus
 giganteus*
Phlox maculata (meadow
 phlox; wild sweet William);
 P. paniculata (perennial
 phlox)
Polygonatum × hybridum
 (syn. *P. multiflorum*)
Primula alpicola; *P. florindae*
 (giant cowslip); *P. secundiflora*;
 P. sikkimensis (Himalayan
 cowslip)
Romneya coulteri
 (Californian poppy);
 R. coulteri trichocalyx
Smilacina racemosa (false
 spikenard)
Tellima grandiflora
Verbena bonariensis
 (purple top); *V. corymbosa*
Yucca filamentosa (Adam's
 needle)

Above: *Not all flowers can be smelt from a distance. You need to be quite close to irises to catch their fragrance.*

Above: *The lily-of-the-valley* (Convallaria majalis) *is one of the best loved of all scented cottage garden plants.*

SCENTED FOLIAGE

Agastache foeniculum (syn.
 A. anethiodora, A anisata);
 A. mexicana (Mexican
 giant hyssop)
*Anthemis punctata
 cupaniana*
Artemisia (wormwood)
Melittis melissophyllum
Meum athamanticum
 (spignel)
Nepeta (catmint)
Salvia (sage)

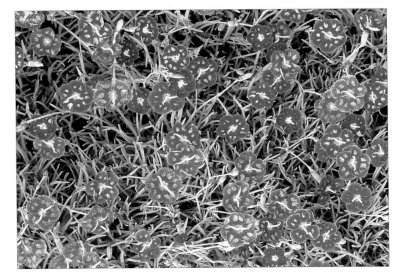

Left: *Old-fashioned cottage garden plants, such as this lupin, are more likely to have perfumed flowers than many of the modern hybrids.*

Above: *Old-fashioned pinks* (Dianthus) *have a wonderful scent, but a short flowering season. A few of the modern hybrids are also scented, but flower for longer.*

Climbing Perennials

When we think of climbing plants, it is usually the shrubby types that come to mind: roses, clematis, honeysuckles and many other cottage garden favourites. However, there are also a number of perennial climbers, some of which can be a wonderfully colourful addition to the garden.

CLIMBERS FOR SHRUBS

One of the most important points to remember about climbers is that they need something to climb up. In the wild, they usually climb up other plants such as trees or shrubs. In the garden, this is not only a possibility, but also a good idea. This is because many shrubs are at their best when they are in flower and, if this happens to be in the spring, then they are dependent on their foliage to provide interest for the rest of the year. So, one way to brighten up a shrub is to grow another plant through it that produces flowers later in the season. Flame creeper (*Tropaeolum speciosum*) is ideal for this, and will happily grow over low shrubs, producing masses of flame-red flowers.

A similar idea is to grow a climbing perennial through another more vigorous climber – the Chilean glory flower (*Eccremocarpus scaber*), for example, will grow through an early-flowering clematis and produce its flowers in late summer and early autumn. Hedges can also be used as supports, as long as the plant is robust enough to stand the competition. Greater periwinkle (*Vinca major*) is ideal for using in this way, and looks superb in spring when its blue flowers peep out from what might otherwise be a dull hedge.

Providing an artificial framework is another way to grow perennial climbers. This is best done in the perennial border by erecting wooden structures such as pyramids, tripods or even simple poles. These provide robust supports which the plants can climb up, or, if they are not self-clinging, against which they can be tied. Most perennial climbers do not grow very high, so the supporting structures do not have to be very tall, and wicker is the perfect material in this instance. Similarly, *Clematis recta*, like many other perennial plants, only needs the help of some peasticks or metal plant supports in order to form a pleasingly rounded shape.

Some perennial climbers are quite vigorous and are suitable for growing over arches or trellises. The golden hop (*Humulus lupulus* 'Aureus') is a perfect example of such a plant. It can also be trained over a framework to make a secluded arbour. However, the stems are rough and can cause serious weals if they rub against the skin, so it is important to make sure that you tie in all the straggling stems.

As a last resort, one way of using perennial climbers, especially if they are not too vigorous, is to leave them alone and allow them to scramble over the ground, forming a loose, straggling pile. Some clematis, such as *Clematis heracleifolia*, are particularly good for this.

Below: *Many perennials, such as these violas and armerias, will scramble quite happily through low shrubs, using them as supports in order to get closer to the light.*

PERENNIAL CLIMBERS AND SCRAMBLERS

Clematis × eriostemon;
 C. × durandii;
 C. heracleifolia;
 C. × jouiniana; C. recta
Codonopsis (bonnet
 bellflower)
Eccremocarpus scaber
 (Chilean glory flower)
Humulus lupulus 'Aureus'
 (golden hop)

Lathyrus sylvestris (perennial
 pea)
Rhodochiton atrosanguineus
 (purple bells)
Solanum dulcamara
 'Variegatum' (poisonous)
Tropaeolum speciosum
 (flame creeper); *T. tuberosum*
Vinca major (greater
 periwinkle)

Above: Clematis recta *is an excellent herbaceous clematis. It can either grow through a low shrub or brushwood supports, or simply be left to form a mound.*

Right: *The golden hop,* Humulus lupulus *'Aureus', puts on a tremendous amount of growth each year, although it takes a few years to reach its full potential.*

Perennials for Ground Cover

Plants that act as ground cover do just that – they cover the ground. For the gardener, there are both horticultural and visual advantages to this. From the horticultural point of view, a plant that covers the ground thoroughly should be welcomed because it will, in theory, help to reduce the number of weeds in the beds and borders. This works on the principle that the plant is so dense that little light can reach the ground and any weed seedlings that do manage to germinate are starved of light, become drawn and sickly, and soon die.

HORTICULTURAL ADVANTAGES

Ground cover is not quite the answer to every gardener's dreams as is sometimes implied. Simply excluding light does not necessarily guarantee that there will be no more weeds. Before planting, it is absolutely essential to make certain that there are no perennial weeds left in the ground. In many cases, even a fragment of root can regrow into a full-sized plant, and no amount of ground cover will prevent this. If perennial weeds do reappear in ground cover there is no alternative but to dig out all of the plants and start again. Therefore, it is important to get the ground completely free of weeds right from the start.

Similarly, if the ground cover is not complete, weeds will simply grow through the gaps. Plants are often recommended as ground cover that are just not dense enough to create total shade at ground level, and such plants are, therefore, useless for ground cover in the horticultural sense. Pinks (*Dianthus*), for example, produce a mat of foliage, but weeds always manage to grow among them. Bear in mind that plants which spread quickly do not necessarily make good ground cover.

VISUAL ADVANTAGES

The other purpose of planting ground cover is to produce a solid mass of one colour as part of a design or colour scheme. For example, a drift of wood anemones (*Anemone nemorosa*) through a wood could be considered ground cover in this context, although the anemones would be useless as weed suppressants.

Allied to this is the use of ground cover plants in order to fill a patch of difficult or unwanted ground. Thus, a drift of *Euphorbia amygdaloides robbiae* could be planted in a dry, shady area to provide some sort of planting because little else would grow there, including the weeds.

When ground cover plants are used, it is often assumed that all the plants should be the same type. This is not completely true. Old-fashioned cottage gardens were often a delightful jumble of plants, planted or self-sown in close proximity. This dense planting still acted as a ground cover, however, even though there was a mixture of different plants. The same principle applies to the modern herbaceous border. Once the clumps of perennials merge in late spring and the ground is covered, the number of weeds that can germinate is greatly reduced. It is only if you leave areas of bare soil showing that you will run into trouble and find that you are constantly having to weed the border.

Left: *The foliage of these hostas provides a very dense ground cover that will help keep weeds at bay, while at the same time looking very attractive.*

DENSE PLANTS FOR MASS GROUND COVER

Acaena
Alchemilla mollis
 (lady's mantle)
Anemone × hybrida
 (Japanese anemone)
Bergenia
 (elephant's ears)
Brunnera macrophylla,
 syn. *Anchusa myosotidiflora*
Convallaria majalis
 (lily-of-the-valley)
Crambe cordifolia
Epimedium
Euphorbia
 amygdaloides robbiae
 (wood spurge)
Geranium × cantabrigiense;
 G. endressii;
 G. macrorrhizum;
 G. nodosum;
 G. × oxonianum

Gunnera
Hosta
Houttuynia cordata
Lysimachia nummularia
 (creeping Jenny)
Maianthemum (may lily)
Persicaria affinis
 (syn. *Polygonum affine*)
Petasites (butterbur,
 sweet coltsfoot)
Pulmonaria (lungwort)
Rheum (ornamental rhubarb)
Rodgersia
Symphytum (comfrey)
Tiarella cordifolia
 (foamflower)
Tolmiea menziesii
 (pickaback plant)
Vancouveria
Vinca minor (lesser
 periwinkle)

Above: Persicaria affinis *provides good ground cover, the flowers (whether in bloom or after they have gone over) as well as the foliage being very attractive for most of the year.*

Above: *The spotted foliage of lungwort (*Pulmonaria*) perfectly sets off the flowers when they appear in late winter and early spring. If sheared over, lungwort will provide excellent ground cover for the rest of the year.*

Above: *The ground-hugging creeping Jenny,* Lysimachia nummularia *'Aurea', works well as a ground cover, as long as all perennial weeds have been removed first.*

Above: *The close planting of any vigorous perennials, such as* Dictamnus, *prevents weed seedlings germinating and surviving.*

Architectural Perennials

Every plant in a border performs a different function or range of functions, contributing to the overall look of the scheme. Some owe their inclusion, at least in part, to their size, shape and sheer physical presence.

USING ARCHITECTURAL PLANTS

Architectural perennials have two roles: one is as individual plants, when they are used to create a focal point, and the other is as a part of the border, when they are used to add to the diversity of shapes and sizes. Focal points in a garden are plants or objects, such as statues or urns, for example, that draw the eye. They can be placed either in isolation – at the end of a path or at the edge of a lawn, for instance – or within a larger arrangement, such as in a border. The eye needs something on which to rest from time to time and one large plant, among many smaller ones, will certainly draw the eye and will probably be the first object the viewer notices.

A cabbage tree (*Cordyline*), for example, with its spray of tapering leaves, placed in an urn at the end of a path will pull your eye towards it so that you appreciate the length and direction of the path. Only afterwards do you draw back and begin to examine the borders on either side of the path. Similarly, a bold architectural perennial, in the middle of a host of other plants in a border, will catch the eye, which rests briefly there, enjoying what it sees, before breaking off and examining the border bit by bit.

On a more general level, a border planted with at least a few architectural perennials is much more interesting than one containing a more uniform planting. Their larger size, as well as the bold shapes of their leaves, adds structure, variety and something striking to look at. However, like most aspects of planting, overdo any one element and the impact is lost.

Strongly shaped perennials often look good in pots or other containers. They can be used in isolation or in groups, and are particularly effective when used as sentinels to a path, steps, a gateway or a door. They also make good plants for patios.

Above: *The biennial or short-lived perennial giant hogweed* (Heracleum mantegazzianum) *is a spectacular plant. However, it should be used with extreme caution as touching it can result in serious skin complaints.*

Left: Gunnera manicata *produces some of the largest leaves seen in gardens. It is bound to catch the eye, wherever it is planted.*

LARGE ARCHITECTURAL PERENNIALS

Acanthus spinosus
 (bear's breeches)
Alcea rosea
 (hollyhock)
Angelica archangelica
 (angelica)
Cordyline australis
 (New Zealand cabbage palm)
Cortaderia selloana
 (pampas grass)
Crambe cordifolia
Cynara cardunculus
 (cardoon)
Delphinium

Gunnera manicata
 (giant rhubarb)
Inula magnifica
Ligularia (leopard plant)
Macleaya cordata
 (plume poppy)
Miscanthus sinensis
Phormium tenax
 (New Zealand flax)
Rheum (ornamental rhubarb)
Stipa gigantea (golden oats)
Telekia speciosa (syn.
 Buphthalmum speciosum)
Verbascum (mullein)

Above: *The red, jagged foliage of the ornamental rhubarb,* Rheum *'Ace of Hearts', can be spectacular, particularly when, as here, it is contrasted with more simple foliage.*

Above: *Angelica (*Angelica archangelica*) can be very imposing, but it is a good plant, not only for the herb garden, but also for the wilder parts of the garden.*

Perennials for Foliage

Perennials are often valued purely for the beauty of their flowers. In a well-designed garden, however, their foliage is likely to play an equally important role. Indeed, foliage usually provides the structure and backbone of the whole border, giving greater solidity to the planting scheme.

THE VALUE OF FOLIAGE

If you were to remove all of the foliage from your garden, you would be left with just a few spots of colour. If these spots of colour were seen against one another, or against bare earth, they would not look particularly attractive. However, if you were to place these colours against a sympathetic background of foliage, the picture would be suddenly complete. Foliage helps to bring out the colours in flowers as well as to meld them together.

FOLIAGE SHAPES

Foliage is important because it brings shape, texture and colour to the garden. Of these attributes, shape is the most significant. The strap-shaped leaves of plants such as grasses and irises, for example, have a quite different quality from the large leaves of, say, an ornamental rhubarb (*Rheum*). The shape of a whole plant, which is often dictated by the foliage, also plays a part. Most grasses are tall and often grow in clumps, with the leaves forming the shape of a fountain. Irises, on the other hand, are more upright and have quite a different appearance. Some plants form hummocks; others make flat mats. The interplay of these different shapes is important to the design of a border.

FOLIAGE TEXTURES

Texture is often overlooked in a garden, but it can play a very important role. Plants with shiny leaves, for example, are valuable in shady areas, where they reflect the light, brightening up what would otherwise be a dark corner. On the other hand, velvety leaves absorb the light and give an impression of richness and luxury. There is a world of difference, both in appearance and feel, between the silky leaves of an artemisia and the rough bristles of a gunnera.

FOLIAGE COLOURS

One tends to think of foliage as simply green, but, of course, the range of greens is enormous. In addition, some plants have purple, yellow and even black foliage. These colours can also be variegated in a number of ways. Some are splashed with gold, others with cream; in some the markings are around the edges of the leaves, and in others they are in the centre.

Above: *Light and shadow play beautifully on the foliage of this crocosmia.*

Left: *A group of contrasting foliage shapes, including* Smilacina racemosa *(top left),* Ferula communis *(right) and* Morina afghanica *(bottom left).*

PERENNIALS WITH COLOURED FOLIAGE

PURPLE FOLIAGE

Ajuga reptans
'Atropurpurea';
A. r. 'Burgundy Glow'
Anthriscus sylvestris
'Ravenswing'
Canna 'Roi Humbert'
Clematis recta
'Purpurea'
Cordyline australis
'Atropurpurea'
Dahlia 'Bishop of Llandaff'
Foeniculum vulgare
'Purpureum'
Heuchera micrantha
diversifolia 'Palace Purple'
Ligularia dentata
'Desdemona'; L. d. 'Othello'
Lobelia cardinalis
(cardinal flower)
Phormium tenax
Purpureum Group
(New Zealand flax)
Rodgersia aesculifolia;
R. podophylla
Sedum telephium
maximum 'Atropurpureum';
S. 'Morchen';
S. 'Vera Jameson'
Viola riviniana
Purpurea Group
(Labrador violet)

BLUE FOLIAGE

Acaena saccaticupula
'Blue Haze'
(syn. A. 'Pewter')
Elymus magellanicus
Festuca glauca
(blue fescue)
Helictotrichon
sempervirens
(syn. *Avena candida*)
Hosta

GOLDEN FOLIAGE

Filipendula ulmaria 'Aurea'
Hosta
Humulus lupulus 'Aureus'
(golden hop)
Lysimachia nummularia
'Aurea'
Milium effusum 'Aureum'
(Bowles' golden grass)
Origanum vulgare 'Aureum'
(golden marjoram)
Phygelius × rectus 'Sunshine'
Tanacetum parthenium
'Aureum' (golden feverfew)

SILVER FOLIAGE

Anaphalis (pearl everlasting)
Artemisia (wormwood);
A. 'Powis Castle'
Celmisia
Cerastium tomentosum
(snow-in-summer)
Convolvulus cneorum
(silverbush)
Cynara cardunculus
(cardoon)
Euphorbia myrsinites;
E. rigida (syn.
E. biglandulosa)
Geranium renardii
Leuzea centauroides
(syn. *Centaurea*
'Pulchra Major')
Lychnis coronaria
Macleaya (plume poppy)
Melianthus major (honeybush)
Romneya coulteri
(Californian poppy)
Santolina
Stachys byzantina;
syn. S. lanata (lamb's ears)
Tanacetum haradjanii
Tropaeolum polyphyllum
Verbascum olympicum

Above: *Two contrasting silver foliages: the filigree* Artemisia *'Powis Castle' and the furry* Stachys byzantina.

Right: *The purple foliage of* Anthriscus sylvestris *'Ravenswing', which is overlaid with silver, is strikingly beautiful. Not surprisingly, this plant makes a valuable contribution to many planting schemes.*

USING COLOUR

Choosing a Colour Scheme

Perennials are available in a wonderful range of colours, which gives gardeners tremendous scope when they design their planting schemes. It is important to remember that colour is provided not only by the flowers, but also by the foliage. The range of colours varies from the bright and brash to the soft and muted. If all these colours were mixed together, without much thought, it would be fun for a while, but the border would soon begin to look untidy and unpleasant to look at.

GROUPING COLOURS

Rather than randomly scattering colours, it is much better to use them in drifts, placing individual plants so that each has a harmonious relationship with its neighbour. When this is done, the eye can move effortlessly along the border, enjoying the subtleties of the border as it passes over a thoughtfully blended whole.

This harmonious relationship depends largely on how different colours relate to each other. Artists and designers use what is known as a colour wheel, in which colours that are situated next to each other on the wheel have a sympathetic bond and will work well together. Purple and blue as well as blue and green, for example, look good together. On the other hand, colours on opposite sides of the wheel are contrasting and may clash with each other. Purple and yellow, for instance, are in stark contrast with each other, and a border in which these two colours are close to one another is likely to be jarring on the eye.

There are, however, occasions when combining opposing colours can be used to create a focal point or to add life to an

Above: *Orange and blue are both powerful colours. Used together in a planting scheme, they produce an agreeable tension as is shown by these bright blue agapanthus and orange crocosmia.*

Above: *This unusual juxtaposition of purple and brown works very well and emphasizes the advice that you should always be keen to try unusual combinations.*

otherwise bland scheme. A splash of yellow in a purple border, for example, would certainly draw the eye. Red and green are also contrasting colours, and a plant with brilliant red blooms, such as Jerusalem cross (*Lychnis chalcedonica*), can look extraordinarily dramatic against a dark green yew hedge.

Pastel colours have a romantic quality, and are often suitable for a rather dull, grey climate. Even so, a garden devoted entirely to pale colours such as these can be rather boring. Hot colours – the flame reds and oranges – on the other hand, are lively and will bring a dash of excitement to a border.

Unless you have set your heart on a monochromatic border, the basic principle is to blend colours. If you want to use two colours that oppose each other on the colour wheel in close proximity, you can sometimes find another colour that will link them. Blue and red are in stark contrast with each other, and you may prefer to keep them apart by placing a purple plant between them, which will greatly improve the appearance of the border. Incorporating foliage in suitable colours is often an excellent way of linking and separating blocks of colour.

When you are buying plants, always try to see them in flower if you are doubtful about the colour. If the plant is a true variety, its colour should be fixed in most cases, but plants grown from seed can vary greatly in colour. A carefully thought-out colour scheme can be ruined if plants turn out to be pink or white instead of the expected blue, so take care when you are selecting or growing plants.

Right: *Yellow primroses are charmingly set off by their own green foliage and enhanced by a fountain of yellow Bowles' golden grass,* Milium effusum *'Aureum'.*

Below: *The combination of these perennials, including* Sedum telephium maximum *'Atropurpureum' and* Heuchera micrantha diversifolia *'Palace Purple', makes the most of the beautiful subtlety of their colours.*

Hot Colours

Odd as it may seem, colours have temperatures – some colours, like the reds, are regarded as hot, while others, such as the blues, are seen as quite cold. This phenomenon is most noticeable when you are decorating, because the whole mood of a room can change, depending on whether you are using colours based on reds or on blues. It is exactly the same when you are designing and planning a garden.

THE HOT COLOUR PALETTE

The really hot colours are those that are on the orange side of red. They include the flame reds, the oranges and the golden-yellows. Alter the emphasis, and the feeling also changes. For example, yellows that contain a touch of green, rather than orange, are cool. Similarly, reds that contain a lot of blue are not as warm as a lively, hot orange-red, and caution should be used in mixing the two.

It is possible to create a border containing nothing but red flowers, but it is always more interesting to have one that incorporates other hot colours as well. If it suits your personality, you may even want to fill the whole garden with these bright colours. Particularly in a very small garden, where there is not space to create more than one mood, this can produce a very striking effect. However, most people are more comfortable with a balance of hot and cooler areas. Going to a few lively parties is most enjoyable, but go to one every night and they will soon become a bore, and you will be thinking of excuses to stay at home.

Use hot colours with some discretion. Confine them to one border, possibly as a centrepiece,

but use softer colours in the other beds to ring in the changes and to provide a more tranquil planting area. The contrast will be all the stronger, in fact, if the red border is surrounded by less lively colours. However, many people prefer to use a limited number of hot-coloured perennials in the middle of a less adventurous border, where they will act as a strong focal point.

Hot colours also have a tendency to "advance" – that is, they seem much closer than they really are – so if you want to make a long border appear shorter than it is, plant the hot colours at the far end.

Left: *The Chilean glory flower* (Eccremocarpus scaber), *with its bright orange, tubular flowers, can be used to create a splash of colour against a wall or fence.*

Above: *The crimson-red flowers of the flame creeper* (Tropaeolum speciosum) *look very striking as they weave their way over a bright yellow-green conifer.*

PERENNIALS WITH HOT-COLOURED FLOWERS

RED FLOWERS

Canna
Crocosmia 'Lucifer'
Dahlia
Geum 'Mrs J. Bradshaw'
Hemerocallis 'Berlin Red';
 H. 'Ed Murray';
 H. 'Little Red Hen';
 H. 'Red Precious';
 H. 'Stafford'; *H.* 'Wally
Nance'
Kniphofia (red-hot poker)
Leonotis ocymifolia,
 syn. *L. leonurus* (lion's ear)
Lobelia tupa
Lychnis chalcedonica
 (Jerusalem cross, Maltese
 cross)
Mimulus cupreus
 'Whitecroft Scarlet';
 M. 'Wisley Red'
Monarda 'Cambridge
 Scarlet'
Paeonia (peony)
Penstemon barbatus;
 P. 'Flame'; *P. jamesii;*
 P. 'Rubicundus'; *P. superbus*
Potentilla 'Gibson's Scarlet'
Tropaeolum speciosum
 (flame creeper)

ORANGE FLOWERS

Anthemis sancti-johannis
 (St John's chamomile)
Canna 'Orange Perfection'
Crocosmia (montbretia);
 C. paniculata
Dahlia
Eccremocarpus scaber
 (Chilean glory flower)
Euphorbia griffithii
Geum 'Borisii';
 G. coccineum
Hemerocallis (daylily)
Kniphofia (red-hot poker)
Ligularia (leopard plant)
Papaver orientale
 (oriental poppy)

Potentilla 'William Rollison'
Primula bulleyana
 (a Candelabra Primula)
Rudbeckia hirta
Trollius (globeflower)
Zauschneria californica

YELLOW–GOLD FLOWERS

Achillea (yarrow);
 A. 'Coronation Gold';
 A. filipendulina 'Gold Plate'
Anthemis tinctoria
 (golden marguerite)
Aster linosyris
Aurinia saxatilis,
 syn. *Alyssum saxatile*
 (gold dust)
Bupthalmum salicifolium
Canna
Centaurea
 macrocephala
Chrysanthemum
Coreopsis verticillata
Dahlia
Erysimum 'Bredon';
 E. 'Jubilee Gold'
Geum 'Lady Stratheden'
Helenium (sneezeweed)
Helianthus (sunflower)
Heliopsis (ox eye)
Hemerocallis (daylily)
Hieracium (hawkweed)
Inula
Ligularia (leopard plant)
Lysimachia nummularia
 (creeping Jenny);
 L. punctata (garden
 loosestrife)
Oenothera (evening
 primrose)
Primula
Ranunculus
 (buttercup, crowfoot)
Rudbeckia
 (coneflower)
Solidago (golden rod)
Trollius (globeflower)
Tropaeolum polyphyllum

Right: *Kniphofias have several alternative names, of which red-hot poker aptly describes the colour of many of them. These shafts of hot colours are useful not only for their brightness, but also their shape.*

Below: *The flat flowerheads of* Achillea *'Coronation Gold' form a sea of hot yellow, floating above the green foliage.*

Above: Zauschneria californica *has hot orange flowers, but the softness of the foliage tends to take away some of the heat. Soft foliage is often used for this purpose in a border.*

Pastel Colours

If hot colours are jazzy and lively, pastel shades are soft and romantic. They produce a wonderful, hazy effect, which is tranquil and peaceful. The colours in this part of the spectrum include the soft blues, yellows, whites and pinks. They are not the complete opposite of the hot colours, since, in theory, they would simply be the cold or cool colours, but pinks, and those blues that are tinged with red, are warm in temperature. The overall effect, however, is one of cool calm.

COMBINING THE PASTELS

Pastel colours create a misty effect, which means that they can be mixed together and even dotted around. An even better effect can be achieved by using drifts of colour rather than dots, merging or blending one drift into another. Restricting your choice to one specific colour can create an interesting effect, but a border of, for example, only pale blues or pale yellows can look a little wishy-washy, and expanses of these colours should only be used in moderation.

Soft green foliage can provide an effective link in borders and beds filled with pastel colours, whereas dark green, at least in any great quantity, can be too stark. Silver can look stunning when mixed with pinks and pale blue, and, perhaps surprisingly, it can also be extremely effective with pale and greeny yellows. Blue foliage, which can be found in some grasses and hostas, can also be useful in linking or separating blocks of colour.

Many of the pale colours, especially white and blue, stand out well at twilight, and perennials in these colours are particularly useful to plant near an area where you eat in the evening. As the light fades, they will shine out and be seen in ghostly outline, even after it has become quite dark.

Soft, cool colours make objects seem further away, just as, on a misty day, the horizon always seems more distant than it does on a bright day. Designers and gardeners often use this principle in order to make a border seem longer than it actually is, and placing pale colours at the far end of a border creates a surprising optical illusion.

Above: Allium christophii *and* Linaria purpurea *'Canon Went' provide a good combination of colours and shapes.*

Above: *Using soft yellows and whites together creates a more striking, even starker, contrast than the combination of other pastel shades.*

Right: *Cream, soft mauve and softly variegated foliage blend to create a soothing effect.*

PERENNIALS WITH PALE FLOWERS

BLUE–MAUVE FLOWERS

Aconitum (monkshood; this plant is poisonous)
Agapanthus (African lily)
Ajuga reptans (common bugle)
Anchusa azurea
Aquilegia flabellata
Aster (Michaelmas daisy)
Baptisia australis (blue false indigo)
Brunnera macrophylla, syn. *Anchusa myosotidiflora*
Campanula (bellflower)
Catananche caerulea
Delphinium
Echinops ritro
Eryngium (sea holly)
Galega officinalis (goat's rue)
Gentiana (gentian)
Geranium (cranesbill)
Hosta
Iris
Linum narbonense (flax)
Meconopsis (blue poppy)
Myosotis (forget-me-not)
Nepeta (catmint)
Omphalodes (navelwort)
Penstemon heterophyllus
Perovskia atriplicifolia
Platycodon grandiflorus (balloon flower)
Polemonium caeruleum
Primula
Pulmonaria (lungwort)
Salvia (sage)
Scabiosa caucasica
Tradescantia × andersoniana
Verbena rigida
Veronica (speedwell)

YELLOW FLOWERS

Achillea 'Moonlight'
Anthemis tinctoria 'Sauce Hollandaise'
Asphodeline lutea (syn. *Asphodelus luteus*)
Cephalaria gigantea
Coreopsis verticillata 'Moonbeam'
Digitalis lutea (straw foxglove)
Erysimum suffrutescens
Helenium (sneezeweed)
Helianthus (sunflower)
Heliopsis (ox eye)
Hemerocallis (daylily)
Hieracium (hawkweed)
Iris pseudacorus (yellow flag)
Kniphofia 'Little Maid'
Oenothera stricta 'Sulphurea'
Paeonia mlokosewitschii
Potentilla recta
Primula
Ranunculus (buttercup, crowfoot)
× *Solidaster luteus*
Thalictrum flavum glaucum
Trollius × cultorum 'Alabaster'

PINK FLOWERS

Anemone × hybrida (Japanese anemone)
Armeria (thrift, sea pink)
Aster (Michaelmas daisy)
Astilbe
Bergenia cordifolia
Dianthus (carnations, pinks)
Diascia
Dicentra
Erigeron 'Charity'
Filipendula (meadowsweet)
Geranium (cranesbill)
Lamium maculatum 'Roseum'
Linaria purpurea 'Canon Went'
Lychnis flos-jovis
Malva moschata (musk mallow)
Monarda 'Croftway Pink'
Penstemon 'Hidcote Pink'
Persicaria (knotweed)
Phlox paniculata (perennial phlox)
Phuopsis stylosa
Primula
Sedum (stonecrop)
Sidalcea (prairie mallow)

Above: *Pink is a very good colour to use in pastel schemes. These pinks* (Dianthus) *are a particularly good choice because they often have a soft, romantic perfume as well.*

Above: *Mauves and silvers in the foreground combine with other soft colours to create a tranquil cottage garden.*

White and Cream Perennials

White is a symbolic colour, and, since the earliest days of gardening, white flowers have had a special significance. Many gardeners are sufficiently under its spell to devote whole borders to the colour. White imparts a sense of purity and tranquillity, and these are two of the qualities that flowers of this colour will bring to a garden. There is something serene about an area of white flowers that is difficult to capture in any other way. It is a good idea to place a seat in an area devoted to white flowers, because it is the perfect place in which to relax.

THE WHITE GARDEN
In has become fashionable to devote whole borders, even whole gardens, to white flowers. Although they are usually referred to as white gardens, there are usually at least two colours present, because most white-flowered plants have green leaves. A third colour, in the form of grey or silver foliage, is also often added.

It is not as easy as it may seem to create a white garden, because there are, perhaps surprisingly, many different shades of white, and they do not always mix sympathetically. On the whole, it is better to stick to pure whites, since the creamier ones tend to "muddy" the picture. Creams are soothing in themselves, and, with care, a border can be created from them, as an alternative to pure white. Many white and cream flowers, particularly members of the daisy family, have bright yellow centres, and it best to avoid these if you are planning a white border. They do, however, mix better with cream flowers.

White and cream go well with most other colours, and they can be used to lighten a colour scheme. When used with hot oranges and reds, pure white can create a dramatic effect, whereas creams add a slightly mellower feel. White and blue is always a popular combination, and it can be particularly effective to combine different shades of white and cream with a mixture of pastel colours. White is visible until well after dark, and so it is a good colour to plant where you eat evening meals.

Above: *Planting* Arabis alpina caucasica *'Flore Pleno' against the dark purple-brown foliage of* Euphorbia dulcis *'Chameleon' accentuates the whiteness of the flowers.*

Left: *An association of white* Tanacetum parthenium *with* Galega × hartlandii *'Alba'. The yellow centres of the tanacetum flowers soften the stark effect of having so many white flowers*

WHITE AND CREAM PERENNIALS

Achillea ptarmica 'The Pearl'
Aconitum napellus vulgare
'Albidum' (poisonous)
Agapanthus campanulatus
albidus
Anaphalis margaritacea
Anemone × hybrida
'Honorine Jobert';
A. nemorosa (wood anemone)
Anthemis punctata cupaniana
Anthericum liliago
(St Bernard's lily)
Aquilegia vulgaris 'Nivea'
Arabis (rock cress)
Argyranthemum frutescens
(marguerite)
Artemisia lactiflora (white
mugwort)
Aruncus dioicus (goat's
beard)
Aster novae-angliae
'Herbstschnee'
Astilbe × arendsii 'Irrlicht'
Bellis (daisy)
Bergenia 'Silberlicht'
Campanula latiloba 'Alba'
Centranthus ruber 'Albus'
Cerastium tomentosum
(snow-in-summer)
Cimicifuga cordifolia;
C. simplex
Convallaria majalis
(lily-of-the-valley)
Crambe cordifolia
Dianthus 'Haytor White';
D. 'Mrs Sinkins'
Dicentra spectabilis 'Alba'
Dictamnus albus
Echinops sphaerocephalus
Epilobium angustifolium
album
Eryngium eburneum
Galium odoratum, syn.
Asperula odorata (woodruff)
Geranium phaeum 'Album';
G. sanguineum 'Album'
Gypsophila paniculata
'Bristol Fairy'
Hosta

Houttuynia cordata
Iberis sempervirens
Iris
Lamium maculatum
'White Nancy'
Leucanthemum × superbum
'Everest'
Lilium (lily)
Lupinus (lupin)
Lychnis coronaria 'Alba'
Lysimachia clethroides
(gooseneck loosestrife);
L. ephemerum
Malva moschata alba
(white musk mallow)
Myrrhis odorata (sweet cicely)
Osteospermum ecklonis
Paeonia (peony)
Papaver orientale
'Perry's White'
Penstemon serrulatus 'Albus';
P. 'White Bedder'
Phlox paniculata 'Fujiyama'
Physostegia virginiana 'Alba'
Polygonatum × hybridum
(syn. *P. multiflorum*)
Pulmonaria officinalis
'Sissinghurst White'
Ranunculus aconitifolius
(bachelor's buttons)
Rodgersia
Romneya coulteri
(Californian poppy)
Sanguinaria canadensis
(bloodroot)
Silene uniflora, syn.
S. maritima (sea campion)
Smilacina racemosa (false
spikenard); *S. stellata*
(star flower)
Thalictrum (meadow rue)
Trillium grandiflorum
(wake robin)
Verbascum chaixii 'Album'
Veronica gentianoides 'Alba'
Viola cornuta Alba Group;
V. odorata 'Alba'
Zantedeschia aethiopica
(arum lily)

Above: *The flowers of* Crambe cordifolia *create a white haze, a quite different effect from that produced by plants with more "solid" flowers.*

Above: *The clusters of small flowers of* Eupatorium album *'Braunlaub' produce a foam-like effect, rather like waves breaking on a seashore.*

Spring

Although the working year in the garden begins in winter, it is spring that heralds the start of the new flowering season. Because most perennials are herbaceous, they have spent time below ground and now emerge as clumps of new foliage. Some plants, however, will have been around all winter. The lungworts (*Pulmonaria*), for example, have been in leaf constantly and now produce masses of blue, red, pink or white flowers. The hellebores are in full swing, as are the primulas, of which the humble primrose (*Primula vulgaris*) is still one of the best loved.

SPRING COLOURS

As the days begin to lengthen and the air and ground become warmer, the early-comers, such as hellebores, winter aconites and primulas, move into the background as other plants begin to emerge. Indeed, it is a good idea to grow the early plants towards the back of the bed or border so that they show up in early spring, when they are in flower, but then disappear behind later-flowering plants for the rest of the year. Among the next phase of plants are the bleeding hearts (*Dicentra spectabilis*) and other dicentras, which need light shade and will grow happily under trees that have yet to open their leaves. Wood anemones (*Anemone nemorosa*), which are available in a range of white and delicate blues, pinks and yellows, also make use of the temporary light under deciduous trees and shrubs.

At this time of year everything feels fresh. The soil is often still damp, and the foliage and flowers are brightly coloured. One of the most ubiquitous colours of spring is sunny yellow. Apart from bulbs such as crocuses and daffodils, many perennials put in an appearance, including leopard's bane (*Doronicum*), with its brilliant golden daisies, and kingcups (*Caltha*), which are a must for any bog or waterside planting. *Paeonia mlokosewitschii*, one of the earliest peonies to flower, has delicate yellow flowers (which are followed in autumn by scarlet and black seeds). This

Left: *The bright yellow flowers of* Anemone ranunculoides *'Pleniflora' can be used to illuminate a shady spot.*

Above: Euphorbia polychroma *creates a perfect dome, which is effective in any spring border.*

yellow is intensified in association with the acid green of *Euphorbia polychroma*, which forms beautiful mounds.

LATE SPRING FLOURISHES

As spring passes, the number of plants in leaf and flower increases, until, just on the juncture with early summer, the garden almost seems over-burdened and it is difficult to keep pace with the newcomers. At this time of year, the foliage also still looks crisp and lush, before the strong sun drains away its colour and freshness.

Many gardeners like to plant in spring, but it is important not to get too carried away and to plant only those plants that are in flower or of interest at the time. Remember to include some that will provide something to look at later in the year.

Above: *Primroses are ideal for a cottage garden.*

Below: *The purple foliage and blue flowers of* Veronica peduncularis *'Georgia Blue' form spectacular spring carpets.*

SPRING-FLOWERING PERENNIALS

Ajuga reptans
 (common bugle)
Anemone blanda;
 A. nemorosa (wood anemone)
Arabis (rock cress)
Bergenia (elephant's ears)
Cardamine (bitter cress)
Dicentra
Doronicum (leopard's bane)
Erythronium
 (dog's-tooth violet)
Euphorbia polychroma
Helleborus (hellebore)
Lamium maculatum; *L. orvala*

Meconopsis cambrica
 (Welsh poppy)
Myosotis (forget-me-not)
Primula
Pulmonaria (lungwort)
Pulsatilla
 (pasqueflower)
Ranunculus ficaria
 (lesser celandine)
Symphytum (comfrey)
Trillium (wood lily)
Veronica peduncularis
 'Georgia Blue'
Viola

Right: *The delicate flowers of dicentras bring freshness to a spring border. Here, they are planted with forget-me-nots.*

Summer

Summer always seems to arrive unannounced. One minute it is spring, the next it is summer, and the borders are bursting with life. Summer is the height of the perennial year. It is a season of colour and scents, humming bees and fluttering butterflies. It is also a time when gardeners should be able to relax and enjoy the fruits of their labours.

THE STAGES OF SUMMER

Although this season is usually regarded simply as "summer", in gardening terms there is quite a difference between early summer, midsummer and late summer. Early summer carries on where spring left off, with plenty of fresh-looking foliage and bright colours. Lupins, poppies, peonies and delphiniums add to the delights and are vital parts of any display at this time of year.

As midsummer approaches, the colours change subtly and flowers with more muted tones unfurl, including *Catananche* (sometimes known as cupid's dart), penstemons, baby's breath (*Gypsophila*) and phlox.

By late summer the colours are fading and the foliage is starting to look a little tired. The colours begin to swing towards the autumnal ones of deep golds and russet reds, as perennials such as achilleas, heleniums and inulas come into their own.

There are perennials with flowers in all colours throughout the summer, and so you can control the appearance of the borders by choosing whatever colours you need. Some plants flower throughout the season – various hardy geraniums, for example, will supply colour for months on end, and a number of red-hot pokers (*Kniphofia*) can supply displays of red and orange spikes throughout the entire summer and well into the autumn.

BED AND BORDER CARE

As the display changes, it is important that the beds and borders are kept tidy and well-maintained, so that dead and dying material does not mar the appearance of what is currently in flower. The flowers of each plant should be dead-headed as soon as they go over. This not only removes an eyesore, but also prevents the plant's energy from being spent on seed production. Instead, the energy is channelled back into the plant, which may then produce a second, later crop of flowers.

Some plants benefit from being cut right back to the ground, which encourages a flush of new leaves, so they can then act as foliage plants. Lady's mantle (*Alchemilla mollis*), for example, not only looks tired and tatty if it is left, but it also seeds itself everywhere. If it is sheared back to its base after flowering, however, it will produce a set of beautiful new foliage and self-sowing will have been prevented.

Although constant attention to the borders is needed to keep them looking their best, there is little point in producing a magnificent garden if you do not allow yourself any time to relax in it and admire the results of all your labours. Make a point of strolling around your garden, perhaps in company, or, better still, sit back and simply admire what you have achieved. Your garden will more than repay the effort you have put into it.

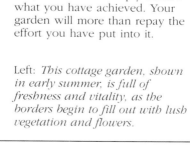

Left: *This cottage garden, shown in early summer, is full of freshness and vitality, as the borders begin to fill out with lush vegetation and flowers.*

SUMMER-FLOWERING PERENNIALS

Acanthus (bear's breeches)
Achillea (yarrow)
Aconitum (monkshood; this plant is poisonous)
Alchemilla (lady's mantle)
Aster amellus; A. × frikartii
Astilbe
Baptisia (false indigo)
Campanula (bellflower)
Catananche (cupid's dart, blue cupidone)
Centaurea (knapweed)
Dianthus (carnations, pinks)
Digitalis (foxglove; this plant is poisonous)
Echinops (globe thistle)
Erigeron (fleabane)
Eryngium (sea holly)
Euphorbia (spurge, milkweed)
Geranium (cranesbill)
Gypsophila (baby's breath)
Helenium (sneezeweed)

Hemerocallis (daylily)
Heuchera (coral bells)
Hosta
Inula
Iris
Kniphofia (red-hot poker)
Leucanthemum
Ligularia (leopard plant)
Lilium (lily)
Lupinus (lupin)
Macleaya (plume poppy)
Monarda (bergamot)
Paeonia (peony)
Papaver (poppy)
Penstemon
Phlox
Rodgersia
Scabiosa (scabious, pincushion flower)
Stachys
Veronica (speedwell)
Viola

Above: *The hardy geraniums are one of the mainstays of the summer border. There is a vast range from which to choose.*

Above: *The achilleas with their flat heads bring an air of calm as well as a splash of bright colour to the summer border.*

Above: *Perennial varieties of wallflower (Erysimum) make colourful subjects for the early summer border, but, unfortunately, they are not perfumed like the ones treated as annual bedding plants.*

Above: *This summer border, with its delightful combination of fresh yellows and greens and the addition of some bright red highlights, has been beautifully planted.*

Autumn

Apart from looking at the calendar, it is not always possible to say when autumn starts in the garden. High summer usually slips quietly into autumn and there is little apparent change, but, as winter approaches, the differences become much more noticeable.

AUTUMN HUES

Autumn can be a beautiful month in the garden. The colours may be becoming more muted, but there are still plenty of bright tones left. Many plants run on into the autumn from earlier seasons – the penstemons and Japanese anemones (*Anemone × hybrida*), for example – but true autumn has its own distinctive flora. The Michaelmas daisies (*Aster*) are one of the mainstays of the autumn garden, as are the chrysanthemums, while ice plants and stonecrops (*Sedum*) are invaluable for attracting the last of the butterflies and bees.

Yellows and oranges are quite common at this time of year, with the coneflowers (*Rudbeckia*) and sunflowers (*Helianthus*) in flower, but there are also deep purple ironweeds (*Vernonia*) and Michaelmas daisies to add variety.

Lilyturf (*Liriope*), with its blue spikes of berry-like flowers, is a good autumn plant. It is useful because it is one of the few autumn-flowering plants that will grow in shade. The toad lily (*Tricyrtis*) and kirengeshoma, which bloom in late summer and early autumn, are also well worth growing. Many grasses are at their best in autumn, especially the large, statuesque pampas grasses (*Cortaderia*) and miscanthus.

AUTUMN MAINTENANCE

It is important to keep on top of maintenance at this time of year. A general lassitude often seems to set in and maintenance tasks are left to the winter. Unfortunately, the dead material often masks plants that are still flowering, so if dead and dying plants are cleared away regularly, the autumn border will look all the better. A few dead stems add to the beauty of the autumn and winter border, however, and the dead stems and seedheads of the sea hollies (*Eryngium*), in particular, are well worth leaving.

If you are planning a major replanting of a border, it is often worth sacrificing a couple of weeks' flowering, so that you can start work on the border in the autumn. This will give the ground an opportunity to weather and any remaining weeds that reappear can be dealt with before planting begins in spring.

Above: *Autumn is a time of rich golds, as this* Rudbeckia fulgida deamii *shows. Its appearance is a reminder that the gardening year is coming to an end.*

Left: *Many of the autumn-flowering sedums are doubly valuable, working well as foliage plants in the summer, before their softly textured flowers emerge in autumn.*

AUTUMN-FLOWERING PERENNIALS

Anemone × *hybrida*
(Japanese anemone)
Aster (Michaelmas daisy)
Boltonia
Chelone (turtle head)
Chrysanthemum
Cimicifuga (bugbane)
Helianthus (sunflower)
Kirengeshoma
palmata
Liriope (lilyturf)

Leucanthemella serotina
Nerine (this is a bulb)
Ophiopogon
Rudbeckia (coneflower)
Schizostylis coccinea
(Kaffir lily; this is a bulb)
Sedum (stonecrop); *S. spectabile*
(ice-plant)
Solidago (golden rod)
Tricyrtis (toad lily)
Vernonia (ironweed)

Above: *Autumn-flowering sedums are excellent for attracting late flying butterflies and bees as well as providing colour for the border.*

Above: *There are a number of autumn bulbs that are usually regarded as perennials. This beautiful, but nearly upronounceable,* Schizostylus coccinea *is one of them.*

Right: *Asters are one of the mainstays of autumn. However, some, such as this* Aster × frikartii *'Mönch', flower over a very long period, from midsummer right through to late autumn.*

Winter

Many gardeners like to hibernate in the winter, not poking their noses out into the garden until the worst of the weather is over. This is a mistake. Not only is there plenty to see and enjoy in the garden at this time of year, but an hour's work done now is worth several later on.

A WINTER GARDEN

Several plants flower in the winter, including a number of perennials. Although it might not be a good idea to fill busy summer borders with them, they can still be grown at the back of the bed where they will emerge later, while remaining hidden during the summer. If you have the space, it is a good idea to create a "winter garden" where you can enjoy these plants in an area specially devoted to them.

If you can, plant beneath deciduous trees and shrubs, where there is plenty of light during the perennials' growing season, but where they will be out of sight for the rest of the year. Even under-planting a single bush will create a small winter garden.

WINTER PERENNIALS

Hellebores (*Helleborus*) are one of the mainstays of the perennial scene in winter. Perhaps they would not be so important if they flowered later in the year, but their flowers are most welcome during the winter months. They are available in a wide range of colours, and there are also an increasing number of double varieties. *Helleborus purpurascens* is the earliest to flower, usually appearing before midwinter, but the so-called Christmas rose (*H. niger*) usually flowers later than this.

One doesn't normally expect irises to be in flower in winter, but the Algerian iris (*Iris unguicularis*) starts flowering in late autumn and goes on until early spring, taking little notice of the weather. Its mauve or purple flowers are deliciously scented. It also grows best in

Above: *Many perennials, such as this houseleek (*Sempervivum*) growing on the roof of a porch, are evergreen, which makes them very useful for providing winter decoration and interest.*

Above: *Winter aconites (*Eranthis hyemalis*) are true harbingers of spring. Once they have pushed up through the ground, sometimes even in the snow, you know that winter is almost over.*

poor soil and is a particularly good plant to grow in rocky soil near the house. It is, however, irresistible to slugs, and these should be kept at bay if you want flowers. It is the only winter plant that needs an open position.

The lungworts (*Pulmonaria*) are really spring flowers, but in most years they will flower in winter as well, sometimes in early winter. Primroses (*Primula vulgaris*) often flower sporadically at this time of year, too, and sweet violets (*Viola odorata*) will flower in warm spots, often providing an indoor display for early winter.

WINTER-FLOWERING PERENNIALS

Anemone nemorosa
(wood anemone)
Eranthis hyemalis
(winter aconite)
Euphorbia rigida
Helleborus niger
(Christmas rose);
  H. orientalis (Lenten rose);
  H. purpurascens
Iris unguicularis
(Algerian iris)
Primula vulgaris
(primrose)
Pulmonaria rubra
(lungwort)
Viola odorata (sweet violet)

Above right: *Wood anemones* (Anemone nemorosa) *come through the soil before anything else is stirring, and briefly clothe the ground with leaves and flowers.*

Right: *Many varieties of hellebores and pulmonarias start to flower very early in the year, often before midwinter.*

Planting and Maintenance

Sowing Seed

Growing perennials from seed is one of the easiest and cheapest ways of getting a lot of new plants. The techniques involved are not at all difficult, even for those who believe that they do not have green fingers.

The Best Approach

A packet of seed is relatively cheap when you consider the number of plants you will get from it. There is one disadvantage, however. Plants grown from seed do not always resemble the parent from which the seed was collected. If, for example, you collect the seed of a white hardy geranium, with the intention of growing more, you may find that the whole batch of seedlings produces purple flowers. On the other hand, plants grown by vegetative means – that is, by taking cuttings or by division – always resemble the parent plant. Thus, dividing a white geranium will provide white offspring.

Therefore, if you want to produce a bed of, say, a dozen plants, all of a consistent colour, it is best to use vegetative propagation, unless the plant is known to come true from seed. Remember, too, that it is not only the colour of the flowers that may vary: the colour and shape of the leaves, as well as the size and shape of the whole plant, may also be different.

It is not always a bad thing to grow something unexpected, of course. You may, for instance, suddenly get a blue-flowered form from your white-flowered plant, which may be a plant that is not already in cultivation. It is always rewarding to grow something that no one else will have in their garden. In fact, many of the cultivars we see today were originally chance seedlings that simply appeared in somebody's garden. You may be interested in experimenting in this way, or you may simply feel that a slight variation in the colour and size of the plants does not really matter.

Obtaining Seed

There are various sources of seed. Many gardeners rely on the major seed merchants, who produce coloured catalogues listing all their available seed. You will get a much wider choice of plants if you order from the catalogues than if you go to your local garden centre, which can carry only a fraction of the bigger merchants' stock.

Another way of obtaining seed is to join a society that runs seed exchange schemes. These often list thousands of species and include many rarer plants. If you want even rarer and more unusual plants, seeds can be obtained by taking shares in the seed-hunting expeditions in the wild that are often advertised in gardening magazines. These work out to be remarkably inexpensive per packet of seed, but you often have to take pot luck about what is gathered.

Having acquired your seeds, there are two ways of dealing with them. They can be sown in the open ground or in pots. For small quantities and the more difficult plants, pots are preferable, but for bulk growing of the more common garden plants, sowing directly into the soil is far less bother and much less expensive because you will not need to buy pots and compost (soil mix).

Perennials can be sown where they are to flower, but it is more usual to sow them in a nursery bed and transplant them to their final positions when they are large enough to transplant.

Sowing in the Open

Prepare the bed thoroughly by digging the soil and removing all the weeds, then break it down into a fine tilth with a rake. Sow the seed in spring, as the soil begins to warm up. Draw out a shallow drill about 1cm ($1/2$in) deep with the corner of a hoe, using a garden line to keep it straight. If the soil is dry, water, and let the water soak away before sowing. Sow thinly along the row, mark the ends with labels and then rake the soil back into the drill. Remember to water the bed in dry weather and to keep it weeded. When the seedlings have grown to a manageable size, thin them to distances of at least 15cm (6in).

Most species will be ready to plant out in their flowering position during the following autumn.

Left: *Sisyrinchiums are among the many perennials that can be sown in open ground.*

SOWING SEED IN OPEN GROUND

1 Prepare the soil carefully, thoroughly removing all weeds and breaking it down into a fine tilth with a rake.

2 Draw out a shallow drill with a corner of a hoe. It should be about 1cm (¹/₂in) deep. Keep the drill straight by using a garden line as a guide.

3 If the soil is dry, water the drill with a watering can and wait until the water has soaked in before sowing.

4 It is essential to mark the ends of the row, so that you know where it is when it comes to hoeing as well as to identify the plants you have sown.

5 Sow the seed thinly along the drill. Larger seed can be station sown at intervals, which means that there there will be no need to thin.

6 Gently rake the soil back into the drill, covering over the seed. In dry weather, do not allow the soil to dry out.

SEED FOR SOWING IN OPEN GROUND

Agastache (giant hyssop)
Alcea (hollyhock)
Anthemis tinctoria (golden marguerite)
Aquilegia (columbine)
Astrantia (masterwort)
Bupleurum falcatum (sickle-leaved hare's ear)
Centranthus ruber (red valerian)
Corydalis lutea; C. ochroleuca
Delphinium
Digitalis (foxglove; this plant is poisonous)
Foeniculum (fennel)
Helleborus (hellebore)
Lupinus (lupin)
Lychnis (catchfly)
Myosotis (forget-me-not)
Physostegia (obedient plant)
Polemonium (Jacob's ladder)
Primula
Pulsatilla (pasqueflower)
Silene (campion, catchfly)
Sisyrinchium striatum
Thalictrum aquilegiifolium
Verbascum (mullein)
Verbena
Viola

Sowing in Pots

Not everyone has sufficient space to devote ground to seed beds, so it is often more sensible to grow the seed in pots. Another argument in favour of pots is that most gardeners need only a few plants; five plants are usually more than enough, unless you have a large garden or you intend to give them away or sell them.

THE ADVANTAGES

Unlike annuals, which are often needed in quantity, it is usually sufficient to sow perennials in a 9cm (3½in) pot, which will produce thirty or more seedlings. A tray or half-tray will produce hundreds of seedlings.

Whichever method you choose, fill the pot or tray to the rim with compost (soil mix) and then tap it on the bench to settle it. Lightly press down the compost so that it is level. Sow the seed thinly on the compost and then cover it with a layer of fine gravel. Label the pot and water it from above with a watering can or from below by standing the pot in a shallow tray of water.

Place the pot in a sheltered spot, away from direct sun.

There is no need to use a propagator because perennials will easily germinate at normal temperatures, although using a propagator will speed up the process. Germination will take from a few days to two or three years, so be patient. The seed of some perennials needs to have its dormancy broken, and this requires a winter's cold weather before germination will occur. Keep the pots watered.

Most perennials can be sown in early spring. Some, however, such as primulas and hellebores, need to be sown fresh – that is, as soon as the seed ripens – which usually means sowing in late summer or autumn.

Below: *Primula seed needs to be sown as soon as it has ripened.*

1 The equipment you will need to sow the seed includes a selection of pots or trays, a good-quality sowing compost (soil mix), a propagator (optional), and your choice of perennial seed.

2 Fill a pot or tray with compost. Tap on the bench to settle it and very lightly flatten the surface with the base of a pot.

3 Sow the seed thinly on the surface. If you need a lot of plants, do not sow thickly, but use several pots or a tray.

4 Cover the seed with a layer of compost or fine gravel. Gravel will help keep the surface moist, as well as make it easier to water in the seed evenly.

5 Water the pot thoroughly either from above with a watering can or from below by standing the pot in a tray of shallow water.

6 Most perennial seeds do not require heat in order to germinate, but the process can be speeded up if the pots and trays are placed in a propagator.

7 After a few weeks, in some cases only days, the seedlings will appear. Harden them off by gradually removing the lid of the propagator.

Above: *A number of perennials, such as hellebores* (Helleborus), *will germinate more freely if the seed is fresh, that is as soon it has ripened, rather than waiting until spring.*

Pricking Out and Hardening Off

Seed that is germinated in pots needs to be pricked out, which simply means that the seedlings are potted up separately. Unlike annuals, which are often pricked out into trays or strips, perennials are nearly always pricked out into individual pots.

THE RIGHT TIME

Seedlings are ready to prick out when they have developed the first true leaves (the first pair of leaves are known as the seed leaves; the second pair are known as the first true leaves) or when the seedlings are large enough to handle. Knock the rootball of seedlings from the pot and gently break it apart so that the seedlings can be easily separated out. Fill a 9cm (3½in) pot with good quality potting compost (soil mix) and make a hole in the centre of the pot with your finger.

Pick up a seedling, holding on to a lower leaf (never touch the roots or stems), and suspend it in the hole in the compost. You should be able to see where the soil level was when it was in its seed pot by the mark on the stem. Line up this mark with the compost level in the pot and, with your other hand, trickle more compost around the roots. When the hole is full, tap the pot on the bench and gently firm down. It is a good idea at this point to label each of the pots with the name of the seedling, as well as the sowing date. Water the seedling from below by standing the pot in a shallow tray of water or from above with a fine-rosed watering can.

To ensure that the seedling will recover from the shock of being transplanted and start growing away, the pot should be stood in a closed cold frame or alternatively kept in a draught-free place in a greenhouse. Once you are certain that the plant has become established, it can be hardened off by gradually opening the cold frame over a period of a week to two weeks, until eventually the lid is left open all the time. If the plants are kept in a greenhouse, they can be set outside for increasing lengths of time over a similar period.

Once the plants have been hardened off, they can either be planted in their permanent positions in the border, or they can be left standing in an open cold frame. An alternative solution is to make a plunge bed. This is a simple frame with no lid, built from wooden planks, bricks or blocks. It is part-filled with sand or ashes and the pots are stood on or partially plunged into this mixture. The plunge bed helps to keep the roots cool in the summer and warm in the winter, as well as providing a small amount of moisture through the drainage holes in the bases of the pots.

PRICKING OUT SEEDLINGS

1 As soon as seedlings are large enough, they should be pricked out. Water the pot an hour or so before gently knocking out the seedlings.

2 Gently break up the rootball, finding a natural dividing line between plants. Split into clumps, dealing with one at a time.

3 Gently ease the seedlings away from each clump, one at a time. Only touch the leaves, not the roots or stems.

4 Hold the seedling over a pot by one or more of its seed leaves and gently trickle compost (soil mix) around its roots until the pot is full.

5 Tap the pot on the bench to settle the compost and then gently firm down with your thumbs. Add some more compost if necessary.

6 Water the pots with a watering can or stand them in a tray of water. Keep the plants covered in a cold frame for a day or so, before hardening them off.

Above: *Yellow-flowered* Verbascum olympicum *and hollyhocks* (Alcea rosea) *make a striking planting combination.*

Taking Stem Cuttings

Increasing perennial plants by cuttings is an easy way to propagate them. If the plant to be increased is a mature specimen, it will usually mean that there is plenty of cutting material, in which case this method can be almost as productive as growing new plants from seed.

SUITABLE PERENNIALS

One of the advantages of increasing plants from cuttings is that the resulting plants are identical to the parent plant. For many plants it is, in fact, the only means of propagation, especially if your chosen plant is a sterile hybrid that does not produce seed and is impossible to divide. Some plants – the wallflower, *Erysimum cheiri* 'Harpur Crew', and many of the pinks (*Dianthus*), for example – have continued to be propagated in this way for centuries, and our existing plants are still closely related to the original parents that grew all those years ago. In effect, they still contain part of the original plant.

Not all perennial plants can be propagated from cuttings. Experienced gardeners will often know simply by looking at a plant whether it is possible or not, but the reasons for this are difficult to describe. Most encyclopedias of plants and books on propagation indicate those that can be propagated in this way, so you can consult these, or simply learn by trial and error.

Above: *Monkey flowers (*Mimulus*) are among those perennials that can be propagated by taking stem tip cuttings.*

HOW TO TAKE CUTTINGS

Most cuttings are taken in spring and summer, but many plants can be rooted at any time of the year. Penstemons are a good example of this.

The procedure for taking cuttings is straightforward. Pieces of stem are removed from the plant, trimmed up, placed in damp cutting compost (planting mix) and left in a closed environment until they have rooted. The cuttings are then potted up and treated as any other young plants. Stem cuttings can be taken either from the tip of a mature stem or from the new growth at the base of a plant, in which case they are called basal cuttings.

Cuttings should generally be about 10cm (4in) long. In most cases it is the top of the stem that is used, but in some cases – penstemons, for example – any part of the stem can be used as long as it is not too woody. Always choose shoots that are not in flower or carrying flowerbuds.

Once the cutting is removed from the plant, it should be placed in a polythene bag to keep it fresh and to prevent wilting. As soon as possible, remove the cuttings one by one from the bag and prepare them by using a sharp knife to cut through the stem just below a leaf node – that is, where the leaf joins the stem.

Most of the leaves should then be neatly trimmed off, tight to the stem, leaving just the top pair or, if they are small, two pairs. The cutting is then placed in a pot of cutting compost. It has been found that cuttings root better if they are arranged around the edge of the pot. Several cuttings can be placed in

the same pot – as many as twelve in a 9cm (3½in) pot – as long as they do not touch.

Some gardeners first dip the bottom of the cutting into a hormone rooting powder or liquid, although most perennials will root quite satisfactorily without this. An advantage of rooting compounds is that they usually contain a fungicide, which reduces the risk of rotting. Rooting compounds quickly lose their efficacy, and it is important to buy new stock every year.

PERENNIALS FROM STEM TIP CUTTINGS

Argyranthemum frutescens (marguerite)
Cestrum parqui
Clematis
Dianthus (carnations, pinks)
Diascia
Erysimum (wallflower)
Euphorbia (spurge; some)
Gazania (treasure flower)
Geranium (cranesbill; some)
Helichrysum petiolare (liquorice plant)
Lavatera (tree mallow)
Lobelia
Lythrum (purple loosestrife)
Malva (mallow)
Mimulus (monkey flower, musk)
Osteospermum
Parahebe perfoliata
Pelargonium
Penstemon
Phygelius
Salvia (sage)
Sphaeralcea (globe mallow)
Stachys coccinea
Trifolium pratense (red clover)
Verbena
Viola
Vinca (periwinkle)

TAKING STEM TIP CUTTINGS

1 Take cuttings from the tips of the stems and put them in a polythene bag. The length of the cuttings will vary, depending on the subject, but take about 10cm (4in).

2 Trim the cuttings to just below a leaf joint, and then remove most of the leaves and side-shoots, leaving just two at the top.

3 Place up to twelve cuttings in a pot of cutting compost (planting mix) or a 50:50 mixture of sharp sand and peat or peat substitute.

4 Water well, and cover the pot with the cut-off base of a soft-drinks bottle. This makes a perfect substitute for a propagator.

5 A heated propagator will speed up the rooting process. Several containers can be placed in the same unit.

AFTERCARE

Once the cuttings have been inserted into the compost (soil mix), label and water the pot, which should then be placed in a propagator or cold frame. A heated propagator, especially one that is heated from the bottom, will speed up the rooting process but it is by no means essential – any closed environment will suffice: you could simply use a polythene bag, as long as the cuttings do not touch the sides.

Leave the cuttings in the propagator until they have rooted. This will be evident when roots appear at the drainage holes at the bottom of the pot. At this stage, pot up the cuttings individually and grow them on.

BASAL CUTTINGS

These cuttings are struck in exactly the same way as stem tip cuttings except they are taken from the new growth at the base of the plant rather than from a mature stem. Although basal cuttings are often taken in the spring, when the plant first gets into growth, they can also be taken at other times of the year, simply by shearing over the plant. This removes all the older growth and encourages new shoots to start from the base. This new growth provides the material for the cuttings.

Taking basal cuttings is a useful method for increasing most asters, as well as violas, anthemis and nepetas. Other perennials that can be increased in this way are achilleas, phlox and dahlias.

TAKING BASAL CUTTINGS

1 Take short cuttings from the new growth at the base of the plant. Place the cuttings in a polythene bag until they are required.

2 Trim the base of the cuttings. Cut through the stem just below a leaf joint and then remove all the leaves, except for a few at the top.

Above: *Lupins (Lupinus), with their racemes of pea-like flowers, can be propagated by taking basal cuttings.*

3 Place the cuttings in a pot of cutting compost (planting mix) made up of 50:50 sharp sand and peat or peat substitute. You can grow up to twelve in a pot.

4 Label the pot so that you will remember what the plants are, as they may all look the same. Also include the date on which you took the cuttings.

5 Water the pot and place it in a propagator. You can use a polythene bag, but ensure that no leaves are touching the polythene. Seal with an elastic band.

6 When the roots of the cuttings appear at the drainage holes of the pot, gently remove the contents.

7 Although this well-rooted cutting is shown here on the hand, it is best to avoid touching young roots if possible.

8 Pot up the rooted cuttings in individual pots, using a good quality potting compost. Keep covered for a few days and then harden off.

PERENNIALS FROM BASAL CUTTINGS

Achillea (yarrow)
Anthemis
Artemisia (wormwood)
Aster (Michaelmas daisy)
Campanula (bellflower)
Chrysanthemum
Crambe
Dahlia
Delphinium
Diascia
Epilobium (willowherb)
Gaillardia (blanket flower)
Helenium (sneezeweed)
Knautia
Lupinus (lupin)
Lychnis (catchfly)

Lythrum (purple loosestrife)
Macleaya (plume poppy)
Mentha (mint)
Monarda (bergamot)
Nepeta (catmint)
Perovskia (Russian sage)
Phlox
Platycodon (balloon flower)
Salvia (sage)
Scabiosa (scabious, pincushion flower)
Sedum (stonecrop)
Senecio (some)
Solidago (golden rod)
Verbena
Viola

Taking Root Cuttings

As anyone who has accidentally left a section of root in the ground from a dandelion or dock while weeding will know only too well, it is possible to grow some plants from a small piece of root. This is not a large group of plants, but for some, such as named pasqueflowers (*Pulsatilla*) and oriental poppies (*Papaver orientale*), it is the only satisfactory method of reproduction.

PERENNIALS FOR INCREASING BY ROOT CUTTINGS

Acanthus (bear's breeches)
Anchusa (alkanet)
Anemone × *hybrida*
 (Japanese anemone)
Campanula
 (bellflower; some)
Catananche (cupid's dart,
 blue cupidone)
Echinops (globe thistle)
Eryngium (sea holly)
Gaillardia (blanket flower)
Geranium (cranesbill; some)
Gypsophila (baby's breath)
Limonium (sea lavender)
Macleaya (plume
 poppy)
Mertensia
Morisia monanthos
Ostrowskia magnifica
 (giant bellflower)
Papaver orientale
 (oriental poppy)
Phlox
Primula denticulata
 (drumstick primula)
Pulsatilla (pasqueflower)
Romneya (Californian
 poppy)
Stokesia laevis
Symphytum (comfrey)
Trollius (globeflower)
Verbascum (mullein)

SUITABLE PLANTS
Because it is a vegetative method of propagation, the plants grown from root cuttings will be identical to the parent. The plants from which such cuttings are taken are generally those with thick, fleshy roots, especially those with taproots. Often there is no other way of propagating these plants, because division is impossible and stem cuttings do not work. Seed can often be taken, but there is no guarantee that the plants will resemble the parent.

The best time to take root cuttings is during the plant's dormant period, which normally means the winter, and because growth often starts below ground well before the end of winter, the usual time for taking such cuttings is early winter.

Usually the plant to be propagated is dug up and the roots detached, but it is possible to dig down the side of a plant and remove one or two roots, without disturbing the whole plant. This is the safest way of dealing with a precious plant. Remove a root by cutting directly across it at right angles. Then trim the lower end with a slanting cut at about 45 degrees so that it is about 5cm (2in) long. The purpose of making these two distinct cuts is to make it obvious which is the top and which is the bottom of the cutting. This is important because there may be no distinguishing marks, and it is all too easy to plant them upside down by accident.

Fill a pot with cutting compost (planting mix) and firm it down by tapping it on a bench or table. Make a vertical hole with a pencil or piece of dowel and slip the cutting into it, making certain that the horizontal cut is at the top, which should be just below the surface of the compost. Several roots can be placed in one pot.

Water and set the pot in a cold frame for the winter. With the coming of spring, shoots should appear above the compost and closer examination should reveal new roots beginning to appear on the cutting. Once you are sure that there are roots, pot them up in individual pots and treat as any new young plant.

Above: *The elegant* Acanthus spinosus *is among those perennials that can be propagated by taking root cuttings. The pale mauve and white flowers appear in summer.*

Above: *Primulas, in this case a candelabra primula, can be increased by taking root cuttings.*

TAKING ROOT CUTTINGS

1 Carefully dig the plant from the ground, ensuring that the thicker roots come out intact.

2 Wash the soil from the roots and then remove one or more of the thicker ones.

3 Cut the roots into 5–8cm (2–3in) lengths with a horizontal cut at the top and a slanting cut at the bottom.

4 Fill the pot with a cutting compost (planting mix) and insert the cuttings vertically with the horizontal cut at the top, so that they are just level with the surface.

5 Cover the compost and the top of the cuttings with a layer of fine grit. Water and place in a cold frame.

Division

The division of perennial plants is one of the easiest and most frequently used methods of propagation. It is done not only to produce new plants, but also as a means of keeping existing plants healthy and free from congestion. The basic idea behind division is that the plants involved do not have a single root, but a mass of roots emerging from all parts of the plant that touch the soil or are actually in the soil. A new plant can be formed simply by breaking a part of the plant away with some roots attached.

SUITABLE CANDIDATES

A large number of perennials can be increased through division. Most of the clump- or mat-forming plants are easy to divide. A plant can usually be divided if it consists of several "noses" or growing points. Division is another vegetative method of propagation, and each of the divisions will resemble the parent plant.

WHEN AND HOW TO DIVIDE

The best time for dividing most plants is just as they are coming into growth, usually in spring. Some, especially those with shallow, fibrous roots like asters, can be divided at any time as long as they are kept moist during dry weather, but even these are best dealt with in spring.

A suitable time is when you are busy with the spring tidy-up. Any old or congested plants can then be dug up, divided and replanted. This is, in fact, an essential part of the maintenance of many herbaceous plants, which would otherwise die out in the centre of the clump and might soon die out altogether.

Dig up the clump to be divided and work on it in the border, if it is a simple division, or in a potting shed, greenhouse, or at least on a table, if the plant is to be propagated. You will need the young growth around the outside of the clump. The centre is usually old and congested, and should be thrown away.

The simplest way of dividing the clump, especially for tougher plants like asters, is to place it on the ground and insert two forks back to back. When the forks are levered apart, the roots are pulled with it, and you will have two plants. Repeat this process until the plant is in small pieces. This is, however, a rather crude method, and the plant can be damaged, allowing in disease.

Left: *Hellebores can be increased through division.*

SIMPLE DIVISION

1 Water the plant to be divided during the previous day. Dig up a clump of the plant, in this case the Michaelmas daisy, *Aster novi-belgii*.

2 Insert two forks back-to-back into the plant and lever apart by pushing the handles together. Keep on dividing until the pieces are of the required size.

3 The pieces of the plant can be replaced in the bed, but dig over the soil first, removing any weeds and adding some well-rotted organic material.

4 Alternatively, small pieces of the plant can be potted up individually. After watering, place these in a closed cold frame for a few days, before hardening off.

DIVISION BY HAND

A better method is to divide the plant with your fingers. Hold the plant in both hands and shake it so that the earth begins to fall off. At the same time, gently pull the plant apart. Many plants – primulas and sisyrinchiums, for example – seem to fall apart in your hands.

If your soil is heavy and sticky, it will not fall off easily, or, if the plants have very tangled roots, it can be difficult to separate them. However, if you hold the plant under water and manipulate it in the same way, a surprising number of plants will come apart quite easily, without damaging the roots.

Some plants will not separate easily and will need to be cut. Wash off all the soil so that the growing points can be seen and then cut cleanly through the main root that is holding them together. This limits the damage to the plant. Cutting a plant into pieces with a spade will work, but you are likely to cut through so many roots that wounds are left through which infection can take hold.

Larger divisions can be replanted directly back in the soil as long as the weather is not too hot and dry; dull, damp weather is ideal. Firm them in and keep watered until they become established. Before replanting, it is a good idea to remove any weeds and to rejuvenate the soil by digging in some compost.

When a plant is divided into smaller pieces it is best to re-establish the plant by growing it on in a pot before planting out. This is important if you want to sell or give away the plants. Once you have made the division, pot it up into an appropriately sized pot, using a good quality potting compost (soil mix).

Label and water the pot and then place it in an enclosed environment such as a shady cold frame or greenhouse. Make sure that you do not place the pots in direct sunlight. Water and grow the plants on until they are established, when they can be hardened off and then planted out or sold.

DIVIDING BY HAND

1 Dig up a section of the plant, large enough to provide the quantity of material that you require.

2 Hold the plant firmly at the base and shake it vigorously so that the soil falls off and the roots are exposed.

3 Gently pull the plant into individual pieces, simply by manipulating it with your hands. Many plants, such as this sisyrinchium, will come apart very easily.

4 The pieces should now be potted up individually using a good compost (soil mix). Place in a shaded cold frame for a few days and then harden off.

Above: *Some geraniums can be increased through division.*

DIVIDING UNDER WATER

1 Many plants, such as these kniphofias, have very tangled roots or are growing in heavy soils that will not easily fall away.

2 Shake the plants in a bucket of water so that the soil is washed from the roots. Wash with a hosepipe if the soil is very difficult to remove.

3 Once the soil is washed away, most plants break up surprisingly easily into individual sections, each with a growing point.

4 Some plants do not come apart very easily. If this is the case, cut the sections apart with a sharp knife, making certain that each section has a bud.

5 Once the plants have been cleaned and divided, they can be potted up individually and then kept in a shaded frame until they have recovered.

Buying Plants

While growing plants from seeds or cuttings is a rewarding part of gardening, most gardeners acquire plants from elsewhere, either because they buy them or because they receive plants as gifts. There are a few points that should be considered when this happens. These days most plants are sold in containers and are available all year round. In the past plants were sold bare-rooted, and this is still occasionally done today: they are simply dug up when you want them, although such plants are usually available only between late autumn and early spring.

PLANT SUPPLIERS

If you want good-quality plants that are accurately labelled, it is essential to go to a reputable source. Many roadside nurseries that sell just a few plants may offer good bargains, but the plants frequently turn out to be different to what you had expected, especially if there is no label. There is nothing more disappointing than to discover you have bought the wrong plant.

Check your prospective purchase carefully. Reject any plant that is diseased, looks drawn or is harbouring pests.

If possible, knock it out of its pot and look at the roots. Again reject any that show signs of pests. Also reject any that are pot-bound – that is, the roots are wound round and round the inside of the pot, creating a solid mass. Such plants are difficult to establish.

Don't always choose the biggest plant, which may well be slow to become established in your own garden. A smaller, well-proportioned one is more likely to settle down quickly. On the other hand, do not select the smallest ones, because they may

not develop fully. If you are in doubt about the colour of a particular plant, do not buy it until you see it in flower. If the plants for sale are in a greenhouse or tunnel, harden them off when you get them home. Planting them straight out in the garden may put them under stress, from which they might not recover.

A wider selection of plants is available if you buy through mail order, and increasing numbers of reputable nurseries are providing this service. Order well in advance because plants sell out. If you are likely to be away when the plants arrive, give the nursery a suitable date, so that it does not dispatch the plants before you are ready to deal with them. A parcel of plants that has been sitting on a doorstep in full sun is a sorry sight indeed.

As soon as the plants are delivered, put them into a cool greenhouse or other sheltered place, out of the sun, in order to allow them to recover. If necessary, pot them on before eventually hardening them off and planting them out.

Above: *A wonderful stand of delphiniums, protected by a hedge as well as staking that is discreetly hidden below the foliage.*

TIPS ON BUYING PLANTS

1 Most plants are now bought in pots. Always check that the plant is healthy, and free from pests or disease.

2 It is advisable to check if the plant is pot-bound, although this can be difficult in a garden centre, for example. A plant such as this will have great difficulty in spreading its roots and growing properly.

3 It is possible to buy plants in modules, such as this, but they do not give the plants much room to grow, and are better for annuals.

4 Traditionally, plants were bought bare-rooted, that is they were dug up when they were needed. Only buy bare-rooted plants between late autumn and early spring.

Preparing the Ground

There can be no doubt that the soil is the most important ingredient when it comes to creating a garden. Understanding your soil and treating it with care and attention will reap rewards that are impossible to achieve in any other way.

CLEARING THE GROUND

The first task when starting any garden is to clear the ground. The most likely problem will be weeds, but in many new gardens there will be builder's rubbish, such as bricks, and, worse still, discarded plaster, which can cause problems by making the soil very alkaline. This may not be a problem if you already live on a chalky (alkaline) soil, but it can be a nuisance if you have a neutral or acid soil and want to grow ericaceous and other acid-loving plants.

If you have recently acquired an older garden, you may well find that all manner of rubbish has been dumped in it over the years by previous owners who were not gardeners. Do not make a half-hearted attempt to get rid of this. Hire a skip, if necessary, and have it all taken away. It may seem a lot of trouble, but once it is done you will be rid of the problem. If you leave rubbish lying around at this stage it will be more difficult to deal with once the garden is planted.

DEALING WITH WEEDS

The next problem is the weeds. Perennials are often in the soil in the same place for several, if not many, years, and if weeds, perennial ones in particular, find their way into the roots of these plants the only sure way of getting rid of them is to dig up the plant as well. If you don't do this, but simply break the weeds off where they enter the plant, they will soon revive and you will have a constant battle on your hands. More people give up gardening or are bored by it because of weeds than for any other reason.

You must get rid of all the weeds properly. There is no point in just scraping them off the surface because they will quickly regenerate from the remaining roots. They have to be either totally removed or killed. If the soil in your garden is light and crumbly, it is possible to remove the weeds as you dig. On heavier soils you can either cover the ground with an impermeable mulch such as thick black polythene for several months, or use a weedkiller. Most gardeners are now rightly unwilling to use too many chemicals in the garden, but, if it is done properly, it will only need to be done once. Always follow the manufacturer's instructions to the letter.

Dig the soil, adding as much well-rotted organic material as possible. If you can, carry out this digging in the autumn and leave the ground until spring before planting. If you do this you will see, and be able to remove, any weeds that have regrown from roots that were missed before.

GROUND PREPARATION

1 Since perennial beds will be basically undisturbed for many years, it is important to clear the area of any weeds by spraying with weedkiller.

2 You can also clear the area of weeds by organic means, either by skimming off the surface or covering it with black polythene for several months.

3 Dig the first trench to one spade's depth across the plot and barrow the soil you have removed to the other end of the plot.

4 Fork a layer of well-rotted compost or manure into the bottom of the trench to improve the soil structure and to provide nutrients for the plants.

5 Dig the next trench across the plot, turning the soil on to the compost in the first trench. Add compost to the new trench and then dig the next.

6 Continue down the border until the whole of the surface has been turned. Add some compost to the final trench and then fill it in with the earth taken from the first.

7 If possible, dig in the autumn and allow the winter weather to break down the soil. In spring, take out any resprouted weeds and rake over the bed.

Conditioning the Soil

It is impossible to keep taking from the soil without putting something back. Nature does this all the time, and it is important to emulate this in the garden. In the wild, plants are constantly dying back or dropping their leaves, and as they do so, the previous year's lush green growth decays and rots down, returning the nutrients to the soil. In the normal course of things, little is removed from the cycle and plants have a constant supply of the nutrients that are vital to their health and growth.

RECYCLING GARDEN WASTE

In a garden, however, the careless gardener discards all the old foliage and stems into the dustbin (garbage can) or burns it, and it is not returned to the soil to become available for future generations of plants. Unless action is taken to redress this, the soil becomes impoverished and plants become thin and sickly, and are difficult to grow.

The prudent gardener, on the other hand, recycles as much as possible by composting all garden waste and then spreading or digging it into the ground to return it to the soil. Because gardeners remove some of the plant material in the way of cut flowers or vegetables, they should introduce extra material, such as farmyard manure, to supplement the garden compost. In this way, the plants are provided with the nutrients that they need.

SOIL STRUCTURE

Another important aspect to consider is the structure of the soil. Heavy, compacted soils are not particularly good for growing plants. On the other hand, light,

sandy ones also have their problems in that they tend to dry out quickly and the nutrients are leached (washed) out during wet weather. With both extremes of soil type, it is important that the structure of the soil is modified to provide the best possible conditions. Fortunately, this is possible, although in the more extreme circumstances it will take a number of years before the benefits are really seen.

SOIL NUTRITION

To some extent, feeding and conditioning the soil can be achieved in the same way. The addition of rotted organic material not only provides nutrients but also helps to retain moisture and at the same time it helps to break down the structure of the heavier soils.

It is important that the material is well rotted before it is added to the garden, because waste material actually requires nitrogen during the breaking-down process, and, if it is not sufficiently broken down, it will extract nitrogen from the soil so that it can complete the process; this is the reverse of what the gardener wants.

Above: *By providing the best possible soil conditions, you will enable a wide range of plants to flourish, even when closely planted in a border, producing a magnificent display of blooms.*

ADDING HUMUS

1 As much well-rotted compost or farmyard manure as possible should be added to the bed, especially at the time that it is dug.

2 For an existing bed, top-dress the soil with a good layer of well-rotted compost or farmyard manure.

3 Leave the well-rotted compost or farmyard manure as a mulch, allowing the worms to work it into the soil, or you can lightly fork it into the surface.

SOIL CONDITIONERS

Chipped or composted bark has little nutritional value but it is an excellent mulch.

Farmyard manure is rich in nutrients but it also often contains weed seed. Manure also makes a good soil conditioner.

Garden compost, which can be made from all garden waste and the uncooked vegetable peelings from the kitchen, has good nutrient value and is a good soil conditioner.

Leafmould made from composted leaves has good nutritional value and is a good conditioner and mulch.

Peat is not suitable because it breaks down too quickly and has little nutritional value.

Proprietary (commercial) soil conditioners are of variable quality but are usually nutritious conditioners.

Seaweed is rich in minerals and is a good conditioner.

Spent hops, which are the waste from breweries, have some nutritional value and are a good mulch and conditioner.

Spent mushroom compost is good for mulching but usually contains chalk or lime.

MAKING COMPOST

The best material to use when making compost is undoubtedly what came from the soil in the first place – that is, all dead plant material, grass clippings, shredded hedge clippings and prunings. This can be piled into a heap and left to rot down, although most gardeners prefer the much tidier method of using a compost bin. These are wooden or plastic structures into which all the garden waste is placed. The bins should have holes in the side to allow in air.

Any garden waste can be used, as long as it is not diseased, and any woody material should be shredded. Do not add the roots of perennial weeds, and make sure that all waste is free of seeds. In theory, the compost should get hot enough as it breaks down to kill these off, but, in practice, it rarely does and they are liable to germinate wherever the compost is spread. Vegetable peelings and other non-cooked vegetable waste from the kitchen can also be used.

Do not use the compost too early; remember that it should be well rotted before being added to the garden. A good indication that it is ready is that it no longer smells or has a slightly sweet smell. The compost should be dug into the soil in the autumn when you are preparing the beds and borders. In established beds, it can be worked into the soil around the plants or left on the surface for the worms to carry down.

OTHER MATERIALS

A good substitute for garden compost is well-rotted farmyard manure if you can obtain ready supplies. This is animal waste, usually mixed with straw or wood shavings, although it sometimes includes hay, which can be a nuisance if it was allowed to seed before cutting.

Leafmould is another useful material. Collect and rot down your own leaves; never take leafmould from local woods, because you will break the natural cycle and impoverish the soil. Spent mushroom compost is also good, especially for top-dressing borders, but it usually has lime added to it, so do not apply it where you grow acid-loving plants.

Fertilizers can also be used to add nutrients to the soil, but they do not help improve the structure of the soil in the same way that fibrous material does. There are two classes of fertilizer – organic and inorganic. Organic fertilizers, such as bonemeal, which are derived from live materials, usually release their nutrients slowly. Inorganic fertilizers are derived from minerals in rock. They are made purely from chemicals, and, although they are quick acting, they tend to get washed from the soil quickly.

Very few gardeners attempt to change the alkalinity or acidity of the flower borders, although this is much more important in the vegetable garden. In extremely acid gardens, however, it may be desirable to add some lime. Check the conditions with a soil testing kit and then follow the dosage recommended by the manufacturer on the packet.

It is more difficult to turn alkaline conditions to acid ones, however, and if you want to grow acid-loving plants you will have to grow them in containers, rather than trying to change the pH of the soil in your garden.

ADDING FERTILIZER

The best fertilizer is organic material because it improves the structure, as well as the fertility, of the soil. However, if this is not available, use an organic, slow-release fertilizer, such as bonemeal, to feed the soil.

Fertilizers

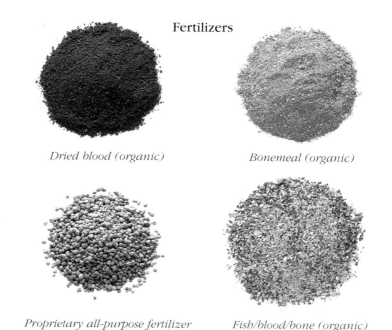

Dried blood (organic)

Bonemeal (organic)

Proprietary all-purpose fertilizer (inorganic)

Fish/blood/bone (organic)

MAKING COMPOST

1 Compost any soft-stemmed garden waste except seed and perennial weeds. Tougher materials, such as hedge trimmings, should be shredded first. You can also add uncooked vegetable waste.

2 Regularly turn the contents of the compost bin and, when full, cover with polythene until the contents have broken down. Alternatively, cover it with soil and plant marrows or courgettes on the top of the bin.

3 The contents should break down, leaving a crumbly, non-sticky, non-smelling compost that is ideal for adding to the soil or using as a mulch.

IMPROVING DRAINAGE

To help heavy soils break down more readily and allow the free drainage of excess water, add sharp sand or fine gravel and fork it into the surface layer.

ALTERING ACIDITY

Although it is not as important as in the vegetable garden, you may need to lower the acidity of the soil. This can be done by adding lime at the recommended dosage.

Planting Out

Planting up a new bed is one of the most exciting tasks that a gardener can perform. There is a real sense of achievement when it is done and a feeling of pride when the bed or border reaches maturity. That the planting never works out quite as one had imagined – sometimes better, sometimes worse – is irrelevant.

PLANNING THE PLANTING

Some gardeners like to pitch straight in with a collection of plants. Others are more cautious and think about the arrangement for a while before they begin planting. While the impulse method may sometimes work, it usually pays to give some thought to how you want your garden to look and what you can do to achieve your wishes.

POINTS TO CONSIDER

The first step is to plan the border or bed. No matter how badly you think you draw, it is always worth trying to sketch out the arrangement of the plants, and at this stage there are several factors to take into consideration. The first important point to consider is, of course, the colour scheme. You should ensure that plants of sympathetic colours are placed together and obvious clashes are avoided. Then there is the question of height. In general, you will want the tallest plants at the back and the shortest ones at the front, but sometimes it is a good idea to add variety by bringing a few of the taller plants forwards. You might also want to mask a section of the border further down the garden, so that the whole border cannot all be seen at once.

One of the other points to bear in mind when planning the design of a bed is seasonal changes. Not all plants bloom at the same time, as we have noted. Therefore, it is advisable to research the flowering times of your chosen perennials in order to spread the flowering from spring through to the autumn, and perhaps include winter, too. Make sure that there are no large areas in the beds or borders that are going to be blank during any of the main seasons – these will only detract from the impact of the other flourishing beds.

Also consider the question of fragrance. Plants that benefit

Left: *The combination of hot, vibrant colours, such as rich crimson, deep purple and sunshine yellow, creates a great deal of impact in this border.*

from being smelt close to, or whose leaves give off a fragrance when they are touched, should be planted near the front of the bed, where they will be accessible.

BUYING THE PLANTS

When you have drawn up the planting plan, try to acquire all the plants before you start planting out. It never seems as satisfactory to plant in batches, because the gaps you leave usually turn out to be either too big or too small. Buy or propagate the plants that you need and then grow them on in their pots, either in a cold frame or plunge bed, until they are needed.

PREPARING THE GROUND

The ground should have been prepared some months earlier to allow it to settle down. Break down any remaining large clods in order to form a fine tilth. Dig out any perennial weeds that have appeared and make sure that you remove every piece of root. The best time to do this is in the spring or autumn, although spring is usually preferable, especially on cold, wet soils. Never work when the soil is wet. Wait until the soil is dry enough for you to walk about and work on it without compacting it. If you have to get on a border when the soil is still rather wet, stand on a wooden plank which serves to spread the load.

If your planting plan is complicated, use string and canes to create a grid over the bed or border. Drawing a similar grid on the plan will help you put the plants in their required positions. Another possibility is to mark the soil by drawing lines on it with sand or peat, which

can be trickled through your fingers or put into an empty bottle and poured out in a steady stream as you move around the outlines.

PUTTING IN THE PLANTS

Put all the plants, still in their pots, in their planting positions. Stand back and walk around the border, assessing the effect and trying to visualize the final result. Some plants will need to be moved because of colour clashes or for other reasons. Others will be too close when they are mature and will need to be moved. A few minutes spent doing this, before you begin to plant, will be time well spent if it avoids you having to transplant something that has grown too large for its position.

When you are satisfied with the positions of all the plants, you can begin to plant. Start at the back and move forwards, making sure that the plants are put into the soil at the same depth as they were in their pots. Water in each plant thoroughly, and then rake through the soil to tidy it up as well as to remove any compaction that has resulted from you having to stand on the soil.

It is rare that everything goes right the first time. There is always at least one plant that is not quite the colour you thought it was going to be and clashes with its neighbours, or one that normally only grows to about 30cm (12in), but enjoys the conditions you have provided so much that it grows to 60cm (2ft) and is in the wrong position.

Some plants languish and never really settle down. It may be necessary to move these, perhaps replacing them with other plants or just moving

everything around. This is best done in the autumn or in early spring. Dig up the plants with plenty of soil around their roots and, after transplanting, water them in well. You will often find that plants that were unhappy in one particular position will flourish when they are moved

Above: Newly planted borders grow away surprisingly quickly.

only a short distance away. The reason for this is often difficult to determine, but there may well have been something in the soil at their first position that disagreed with them.

PLANTING A BED

1 If the bed was dug in the autumn, winter weather should have broken down the soil. In spring, rake over the soil and remove any weeds that have reappeared.

2 Although well-rotted organic material should have been added at the time of digging, a sprinkling of bonemeal will ensure the plants get off to a good start.

3 Draw a grid on a planting plan and then mark out a scaled-up version on the bed, using sand or compost (soil mix). Alternatively, use string stretched between canes to mark out the planting plan.

4 Using your planting plan and grid as a guide, lay out the plants, still in their pots, on the ground. Stand back, and try to envisage the border as it will be, and make any necessary adjustments.

5 Dig a hole with a trowel or spade and, with the plant still in its pot, check that the depth and width is right. Adjust if necessary.

6 Remove the plant from the pot and place in the planting hole. Fill in the hole with soil and then firm the plant in.

7 When the bed is completely planted, water in all the plants. They should be kept watered until they have become established.

8 Go over the border with a fork, or use a rake if there is room. This will loosen any compacted areas, as well as level the soil.

9 Cover the soil between the plants with a layer of mulch like composted bark to keep weeds down and preserve moisture.

10 If you are concerned that you will not remember what the plants are, mark each one with a plastic label.

11 The finished border should need little attention, apart from occasionally removing the odd weed.

Watering and Feeding

Compared with other gardening jobs, watering is generally not an onerous task, and feeding, too, is rarely much of a problem, as long as the ground has been prepared well in the first place. The key to watering is to make sure that the ground contains plenty of well-rotted humus. This fibrous material holds moisture but does not cause the ground to become water-logged.

THE IMPORTANCE OF HUMUS

If humus is dug into the soil, it will hold the moisture down at root level, where it is needed. Spreading more organic material over the surface of the soil will help to prevent evaporation and thus also reduce the need to water. Black polythene (plastic) can also be used as a mulch, but looks ugly and is best covered with another mulch such as chipped bark. Farmyard manure, garden compost, chipped or composted bark and spent mushroom compost are among the best forms of mulch. If humus is dug in and the soil is given a top-dressing, there will be little need to water even in dry weather.

WATERING METHODS

Sandy soil does not retain moisture, and it may be necessary to water in dry spells. A sprinkler of some sort is undoubtedly the most effective method for a border. A dribble hose can also be used. This is a hosepipe with a series of evenly spaced holes in it that slowly releases water. It can be buried beneath the mulch. In a wide border you would need lots of pipes to make sure that all plants receive the water they need. If individual plants begin to flag, a watering can is usually sufficient.

Whatever method you decide to use, always make sure that the ground is thoroughly soaked. If you only wet the surface, you will actually do more harm than good as the plants will tend to form shallow roots, rather than seeking water from deep in the soil. Put a rain gauge or a jam jar within the range of the sprinkler and leave the sprinkler running until there is a reading of at least 2.5cm (1in) of water.

WHEN TO FEED

The same principles hold true for feeding. If the ground is thoroughly prepared in the first place, and then top-dressed with organic material, sufficient nutrients should be available to the plants, and there should be no need for further feeding. Remember that the organic material should be well rotted before it is added to the border, otherwise, in the process of breaking down, it will extract nitrogen from the soil.

Some gardeners who do not have access to much organic material also apply a light feed of a general, balanced fertilizer in spring, but unless your plants are looking particularly starved, there is no need to give them a liquid feed.

1 If they are prepared properly, most borders do not need watering, but in really dry periods a sprinkler is an effective way of covering a large area. Ensure that the ground is thoroughly soaked.

2 Containers are best watered by hand with a watering can. Again, be certain to give the pot a good soaking.

3 Sometimes it is necessary to pep up a flagging border towards the end of a long season. A liquid feed added to a watering can is a quick way to do this. Follow the instructions given by the manufacturer on the bottle.

4 Watering with a hand-held hose is time-consuming, but several manufacturers make fertilizer dispensers that can be fitted to a hosepipe – this is an easy way to supply feed.

5 Early in the season, if insufficient organic material has been used to top-dress the border, a sprinkling of a general fertilizer will help keep the plants in good condition.

Above: *If a border is fed and mulched in spring and autumn, it should not need further watering, except in very dry conditions.*

Border Maintenance

One of the criticisms levelled at herbaceous borders used to be that they required a lot of time-consuming maintenance. This is, in fact, not necessarily true, especially if the ground has been prepared properly in the first place. There are, in addition, some people who actually enjoy gardening, and maintaining beds and borders is part of that enjoyment. Perennial borders require two main types of maintenance, the first during the growing season and the other during the dormant season in winter. The maintenance that is carried out during the growing season is essential in order to keep the borders looking their best.

WEEDING

Some gardeners dislike weeding, but as long as you do not let the situation get out of hand, when you will have an uphill battle, weeding can be a pleasurable activity. If nothing else, it brings the gardener into contact with the plants, providing opportunities to examine them at close quarters, not only to appreciate their beauty but also to check their health and general well-being.

The secret of weeding is to do it before spring gets under way. Whenever the weather permits, go over the ground in winter, removing any weeds and covering the surface with a mulch. In a well-prepared garden this reduces the work for the rest of the year to the minimum. If you leave weeding until the warm weather arrives, the weeds will be ahead of you and be spreading fast, and in these circumstances it is almost impossible to keep them under control. If the ground is maintained properly in winter, it is usually necessary to remove only the odd weed during the rest of the year.

The best method is to weed a border by hand. Avoid using a hoe, which is likely to cut down or damage plants accidentally. Never use weedkiller in a planted border. If perennial weeds do get into the bed, either dig out those plants in the immediate area, and remove the weeds, or make over the whole border.

OTHER TASKS

Many perennials become congested and should be divided every few years. In summer, they also need dead-heading. As the flowers fade, they should be removed. If they are left they produce seed, which uses up energy that is better channelled into plant growth. Dead flowers also look untidy. Many plants can be cut to the ground once they have finished flowering. This not only removes stems that will become more and more tatty as they die back, but also encourages the plant to throw up new leaves, so that it acts as a foliage plant for the rest of the year. Some plants may also produce a second flush of flowers.

SPLITTING CONGESTED PLANTS

1 Some plants need splitting every few years to keep them flourishing. In spring, lift the whole of the clump from the ground.

2 Take the opportunity to thoroughly clean the ground, removing all weeds, in particular any perennial ones that have appeared since the border was last dug.

3 Dig in some well-rotted organic material in order to rejuvenate the soil. Alternatively add some bonemeal, which will help promote root growth. You might like to wear a protective face mask when handling bonemeal.

4 Shake the earth from the plant and divide it into a number of plants. Use only the new growth around the edge of the plant, and discard the woody centre.

5 Replant some of the divisions, making certain that the roots are well spread out. Firm them in and then water.

6 Keep the plants watered until they have re-established themselves. They will soon fill out the gaps.

Staking

One important procedure that should not be neglected, both for the look of the border and the health of the plants, is staking. There are two important factors to remember: make the stakes discreet, so that they are as invisible as possible, and do stake early, before the plants flop.

PLANTS THAT NEED STAKING

Most gardeners find that at least one plant is blown over at some time during the year, and even in sheltered areas, where there is little or no wind, a heavy downpour of rain can cause problems, especially with double flowers, which tend to hold water. Double peonies, for example, have heavy flower-heads, which will often bow down under their own weight. When they are full of rainwater, they topple over as if they were filled with lead.

The key to solving these problems, as with so many aspects of gardening, is to anticipate possible trouble and to stake vulnerable plants before they are big enough to pose a problem. Once a plant has fallen over, it is impossible to stake it in a way that will make it look natural. Plants should always be staked before they are fully grown. This not only affords the plant protection before it is likely to need it, but also allows the plant to grow over its support so that this cannot be seen. Most plants need support between a half and two-thirds of the way up their eventual height, which means that the supports should be in position before the plant reaches half its height. The plant will then be able to grow through the framework.

USING PEA-STICKS

The best staking methods are those that provide some form of lattice through which the plant can grow. One of the most satisfactory methods is to use pea-sticks or brushwood, if available. These twiggy branches are pushed into the ground, right up against the plant. The top twigs are then bent over and interlaced or tied to form a grid through which the growing stems can pass. As the plant grows through the top and sides of this framework, its leaves will cover it, and will eventually hide it completely.

MAKING A CAT'S CRADLE

A similar method is to insert small stakes or canes in the ground and then weave a random cat's cradle of string around them. A more technical method, but one that has the same result, is to use ready-made hoops that have grids of wire welded across them. These are supported on sturdy wire legs at the appropriate height.

Left: *This garden displays a variety of different ways in which plants can be provided with support, including the use of large-mesh wire netting, pea-sticks, and a frame for climbing plants.*

MAKING A CAT'S CRADLE

1 A cheap but effective means of support can be created by forming a cat's cradle of canes and string. Push the canes into the soil around and in the middle of the clumps of plants that need to be supported.

2 Trim off the tops of the canes, so that they will not show above the plants when they are fully grown.

For large areas of plants a similar device can be made by supporting a sheet of large-mesh wire netting horizontally above the plants. The netting can be held in place quite easily, using a series of stakes or canes.

Interlocking stakes, which you should be able to find in most garden centres as well as in many hardware stores, can be placed in any shape, whether regular or irregular, around a clump of plants. A few of these stakes can also be placed horizontally in order to create a grid. They can also be used in a line to provide support for plants that otherwise would flop over a path or lawn. If you do find that you have neglected to stake your plants in time, then these stakes are the best way to lift plants back up again.

STAKING SINGLE PLANTS

All the methods described so far are for supporting clumps of plants. But some tall border plants – delphiniums and hollyhocks, for example – consist of one or a series of vulnerable spikes. These can be staked individually with long canes. If possible, place the cane behind the stem so that it is not so obvious when you are viewing the border. It is rarely necessary for the cane to be as tall as the stem, and a flower stem attached all the way up a tall cane will appear stiff and rigid, giving the plant an artificial look. A better approach is to support the lower part of the stem, allowing the top to move freely. In this way the stake will be less obtrusive, and the plant will appear more natural.

3 Weave string in a random pattern between all the canes so that a mesh of supports is created. At the end of the season, remove the supports from the plants.

A SELECTION OF STAKING METHODS

1 Proprietary hoops with adjustable legs can be placed over the plants. The plants grow through the grid, gaining support from the frame, and eventually hiding it.

2 A good method for supporting clumps of varying sizes and shapes is to use linked stakes that are simply slotted together. These stakes are particularly good for rescuing plants that have flopped over.

USING PEA-STICKS

5 Tall flowering stems can be staked individually by tying them to a cane that is shorter than the eventual height of the plant and hidden from sight behind the stem.

1 Pea-sticks are a cheap, renewable form of support. Push the sticks into the ground around the perimeter of the plants.

3 For larger areas of plants, a sheet of large-mesh wire netting can be supported horizontally over the plants by tying it to wooden posts or canes.

4 Wire netting can also be used vertically to create cylinders, which are held firmly in place with posts. The plant grows up through the centre, with the leaves and branches coming through and covering the sides.

2 Bend over the tops of the sticks at what will be about two-thirds of the eventual height of the plants. Twine and tie the tips together to form a mesh.

3 For climbing plants, such as *Lathyrus*, a tall pyramid of pea-sticks can be created. This will be hidden when the plant attains full growth.

Autumn and Winter Maintenance

A few hours spent working on a border in winter will save many hours the following year. There are a surprising number of autumn and winter days when the soil is sufficiently dry and the weather pleasant enough to get out into the garden and do some work, and you should take advantage of those days whenever you can.

WHEN TO TIDY

Some gardeners like to leave all the work in the garden until spring, and they usually cite two reasons for so doing. The first is that the dead stems can look attractive in the winter; the second is that they provide food and shelter for birds, insects and small mammals. Both points are undoubtedly true, but the rush to get everything done at the start of the year can be something of a nightmare, especially if the spring is wet. When plants have started into growth before you have had time to tackle them, trying to cut back dead stems without damaging the new shoots is far from easy.

On the other hand, if you work steadily through the winter months, not only will you be ahead of the game, you will also save yourself a great deal of work later on. Weeding in the winter means that you have more time to sit and enjoy the garden in the summer.

REMOVING OLD GROWTH

One of the major jobs in the perennial garden is cutting down and removing the old stems from the previous year's plants. These should be cut off as low to the ground as possible with a pair of secateurs (pruners). Rather than burning or throwing away this material, compost it, shredding it first if it is woody, and return it to the soil once it has rotted down. You will need to prune the live growth of some plants, rather than simply cutting off the dead growth. Many of these – artemisias and penstemons, for example – are best left until spring.

WEEDING

Once you can see the ground, the next task is to remove any weeds. Avoid using a hoe because you may accidentally damage shoots that are just below the surface. Weed by hand, using a hand or border fork. When the border is clean, lightly dig between the plants, but avoid getting too close to them, especially those with spreading, shallow roots. Cover the whole border with a layer of well-rotted organic material, such as farmyard manure.

While you are working through the border, take the opportunity to divide any plants that are becoming too congested. Dig them out, divide them and replant them after having taken the opportunity to rejuvenate the soil by digging it over and incorporating humus as you work.

1 It might seem like an impossible task to turn the overgrown mess shown above into an attractive border, but, if you work steadily throughout the winter, the border will be transformed.

2 Carefully cut back all dead stems as close to the ground as possible. As winter passes, more shoots will appear at the base and care will be needed not to damage them.

3 Some herbaceous plants remain green throughout winter. Cut back to sound growth, removing dead and leggy material.

4 Here, the old stems have been cut off so that they are level with the emerging growth, so as not to damage it.

5 Lightly dig over the soil around the plants, removing any weeds. Avoid digging around plants such as asters which have shallow roots.

6 Top-dress around the plants with some organic material, such as well-rotted compost, farmyard manure or composted bark. Avoid using peat.

7 Some plants need some form of winter protection. Here, the crowns of some gunneras have been covered with their own leaves from the previous season.

Dealing with Pests and Diseases

In a well-managed perennial garden, pests and diseases should not be too much of a problem. A variety of plants, keeping a watchful eye and good hygiene are the keynotes.

THE BENEFITS OF VARIETY

The greater the variety of plants you grow in the garden, the fewer pests and diseases you are likely to encounter, because the greatest problems come with monocultures. If you only grow roses, for example, there is lots of food for aphids, and once they start breeding they spread very rapidly, and become almost uncontrollable. Unfortunately, roses are not a home for the ladybirds and hoverflies that prey on aphids, so you may have to resort to chemical controls. In a mixed herbaceous border, not only is the number of plants that will be attacked by aphids limited, but there are also plenty of host plants for their predators, and so a balance is struck and the gardener rarely has to interfere.

Another advantage of the mixed border is that if one plant falls prey to a particular insect or disease, it is probable that its neighbours will not succumb. When blackspot sweeps through a rose garden, however, all the plants are likely to be affected. Thus, diversity in a garden helps enormously to control both the incidence and effects of pests.

KEEPING THE GARDEN TIDY

Good gardening involves keeping tidy the garden, in general, and the borders, in particular. Clearing away dead leaves and dying material will remove the homes and food for many pests and diseases. Compost this type of material before returning it to the border. However, if the leaves are under a plant that has had a fungal disease or if the stems are the remains of such a plant, you should not only remove them but destroy them as well to help reduce the number of spores that can attack again.

Many weeds are hosts to diseases, especially fungal ones – groundsel, for example, is often infected with a rust, which can be transmitted to hollyhocks and other plants. Weeding not only removes the source of disease, but gives you an opportunity to examine the plants in the border. An outbreak of greenfly can be easily checked if you remove the advance guard with your fingers.

If pests and diseases do gain hold it may be necessary to apply chemical controls, but these are rarely necessary in a well-maintained garden. If you need to spray, always follow the instructions on the packet and only spray those areas affected by the pest; do not drench everything in sight.

Slugs can be one of the worst pests that the perennial gardener is likely to meet. You can use bait if you prefer, but going out over several consecutive nights and rounding them up by torchlight usually brings the situation under control.

PESTS AND DISEASES

1 A variety of methods can be used to combat pests and diseases, including netting and black thread to keep off or deter birds and mammals, baits for slugs and snails, puffer packs of chemical dust as well as liquid sprays for insect pests and fungal diseases.

2 Slugs and snails are two of the gardener's worst enemies, particularly in late winter and early spring when new growth can be reduced so much that plants fail to grow. Removing these pests by hand at night is one of the most effective methods of control.

3 Butterfly and moth caterpillars can cause a lot of damage to both flowers and foliage. You can usually maintain sufficient control over the problem by picking the caterpillars off by hand. If necessary, there is a range of sprays and dusts available that can be used instead.

4 Fungal diseases, such as the mildew shown here, are often a problem, especially in either very dry or very wet years. Asters are particularly prone to mildew. Thinning the plants to improve air circulation may help, or you can spray with either a chemical or an organic fungicide.

5 The damage done by rabbits and other mammals can be heartbreaking because they will often browse a plant to the ground. The best form of defence is to surround the garden with a wire netting fence.

6 Although aphids, such as greenfly and blackfly, are among the most common of insect pests, a mixed garden usually attracts enough predators to keep them under control. When serious outbreaks occur, chemical control may be the only solution.

INDEX

ACKNOWLEDGEMENTS

The publishers would like to thank the following for their permission to photograph their plants and flowers for this book:
Hilary and Richard Bird; the RHS Garden, Wisley

The publishers would also like to thank the following photographers for allowing their pictures to be reproduced in this book:

KEY: b = bottom   r = right   l = left

Jonathan Buckley for the pictures on pages 6; 7; 13 (all); 20r; 25 (all); 40 (all); 53b; 56bl; 57br; 59br; 64 (all); 66; 70; 74; 83br

Richard Bird for the pictures on pages 90 (all) and 91br